PRENTICE-HALL
FOUNDATIONS OF MODERN SOCIOLOGY SERIES
Alex Inkeles, Editor

WITHDRAWI

RACE AND ETHNIC RELATIONS

HUBERT M. BLALOCK, JR.
University of Washington

Prentice-Hall, Inc., Englewood Cliffs, New Jersey 07632

Library of Congress Cataloging in Publication Data

Blalock, Hubert M., Jr.
  Race and ethnic relations.

  (Foundations of modern sociology)
  Bibliography
  Includes index.
    1. Race relations. 2. Ethnic groups. 3. Minorities
—Economic aspects. 4. Power (Social sciences)
5. Social problems. I. Title. II. Series.
HT1521.B545   305 .8   81–10536
ISBN 0-13-750182-X   AACR2
ISBN 0-13-750174-9 (pbk.)

Printed in the United States of America

10 9 8 7 6 5 4 3

Prentice-Hall International, Inc., London
Prentice-Hall of Australia Pty. Limited, Sydney
Prentice-Hall of Canada, Ltd., Toronto
Prentice-Hall of India Private Limited, New Delhi
Prentice-Hall of Japan, Inc., Tokyo
Prentice-Hall of Southeast Asia Pte. Ltd., Singapore
Whitehall Books Limited, Wellington, New Zealand

CONTENTS

PREFACE

It is obviously impossible to do justice to a very broad field of study in a single short book, and therefore one must necessarily be highly selective in accord with some assumptions about an intended audience. It is my assumption that this book will be used in one of several types of courses, either in portions of introductory sociology or social problems courses or as one among several books in more specialized courses on race and ethnic relations or perhaps in ethnic studies programs.

In either case, I believe it is essential to stress that the study of race and ethnic relations cannot realistically be isolated from many other closely related social phenomena. For this reason, I have attempted to work into the discussion a number of rather general sociological ideas. In particular, I have stressed that race relations represent special types of intergroup processes that require for their understanding some knowledge of history, economics, political science, and social psychology, as well as sociology. Although I have attempted to avoid many of the "big words" and confusing terminology that, to some, characterize sociological theory, I have stressed throughout that important theoretical ideas and issues can be applied to the study of race and ethnic relations.

This very practical field of study provides an excellent opportunity to test and reformulate many ideas relating to such diverse theoretical issues as the relationship between attitudes and behaviors, the role of power and conflict, the complexity of class relationships, the interplay between economic and political systems, the validity or invalidity of Marxist analyses, and many other theoretical issues that crosscut sociology and the other social sciences. Thus the study of race and ethnic relations provides an excellent way of introducing the student to a wide range of important sociological issues, as well as studying one of our most serious social problems.

Thus the orientation of this book is rather more theoretical than detail-factual in nature. In particular, I have tried to avoid concentrating on specific minorities, or on quantitative information about their present social, economic, and political situations, and have instead attempted to approach the subject from a somewhat less "dated" perspective. At the same time, I recognize that some undergraduates will be coming to the subject with much more specific information about some minorities than others. Many will have a much greater interest in the present than the past. Therefore, I have supplied some such current information, while stressing the operation of much more long-term and more macro-level processes than are of immediate concern to those with highly applied interests. I do this because, like many sociologists, I believe that effective action requires intelligent understanding that is based on theoretical generalizations, or rudimentary laws, that transcend these immediate situations.

It is also my belief that a theoretical "roadmap" is absolutely essential in this very diffuse area of study. Without such a roadmap, the student is very likely to wander aimlessly, or perhaps locate his or her efforts within a very restricted terrain. In either case, without some concern for the "big picture," it is extremely easy to be led astray, or to follow an overly narrow path that ends somewhere other than where one has intended. Furthermore, if we all follow these narrow paths we are more likely than not to talk past one another, proposing "solutions" that are either overly simplistic or fundamentally at odds with one another.

In addition to this effort to introduce some theoretical ideas, I have also provided a few sections that some readers may consider technical. I do so because much of the literature on these topics *is* somewhat technical, and we do our students a disservice if we do not encourage them to discover this fact about some of the sociological literature. But I also do so because I believe that, in many instances, somewhat technical analyses are very much needed to disentangle complex causal processes that are at work. We therefore need, even in very introductory discussions, to expose these students to some of these complexities, as for example those that are discussed in Chapter 5 in connection with the status-attainment literature.

CHAPTER 1
INTRODUCTION

Racial and ethnic relations are a special type of intergroup relations. Almost always they involve power relationships in which a dominant group allocates to itself the greater share of rewards, such as the best jobs and housing, and of control over the most important resources or centers of power. Relations between racial and ethnic groups need not involve overt conflict, and, indeed, instances of violence are likely to be relatively rare. Yet when conflict does occur, the severity and sadism involved may almost defy rational explanation. Often the relationship between such groups is likely to involve either extremely unequal rates of exchange or—if the minority is too unimportant to be of service, or if unskilled labor is no longer needed—a virtual neglect of the weaker party.

Those who study this field must be prepared to encounter some disturbing facts. Some are well known to most Americans. If one belongs to one of our own current minorities, some of these facts will have been experienced first hand, with the result that one is likely to perceive such phenomena as being unique or as being more relevant to one's own group than to other minorities. Yet they are not unique. Consider the following as illustrative evidence:

—Approximately six million Jews were systematically exterminated by the Nazis during World War II. Prior to this the Hitler regime conducted a carefully conceived program, supported by the overwhelming majority of the German public, to identify all persons with Jewish ancestry, to remove them from the most desirable occupations and professions, to incite mob violence against them, and to transfer them to forced labor camps.

—For a period of several hundred years, British, French, Spanish, and Portuguese ships sailed the Atlantic with human cargoes of slaves packed into their holds. Millions died in the passage. Yet it was not until slavery became unprofitable that "sentiment" turned against this slave trade.[1]

—The American government has broken treaty after treaty made with a wide diversity of American Indian tribes. It has relegated them to smaller and smaller parcels of land deemed useless to white settlers and has failed to protect them from senseless slaughter as well as encroachments on this land.

—In 1942, shortly after the Japanese attack on Pearl Harbor, American citizens of Japanese ancestry—as well as their immigrant parents who had been prevented by law from becoming citizens—were rounded up, deprived of their property, and removed to what amounted to American versions of concentration camps.[2] Yet no Americans of German or Italian ancestry were similarly treated.

—In Japan, there is a minority population known as the Eta. The Eta have been treated as an "outcast" group and discriminated against to at least as great a degree as blacks have been in the United States. Yet the Eta are not racially distinct from other Japanese.

—The Chinese in South Asia, and certain Asian minorities in Africa, have played roles similar to those of such "middle-class minorities" as the Jews and Japanese-Americans in the United States. They have been stereotyped in much the same way and have been persecuted during times of crisis.[3] It is probably no coincidence that a very high percentage of the refugees from Vietnam are ethnic Chinese.

—The colonialist policies once followed by European governments in both Africa and Asia totally ignored ethnic and political differences within the colonized territories. As a result, when new African and Asian nations were created, little regard was given to the rights of ethnic and racial minorities within these new nations. The Nigerian civil war, in which millions of Ibo tribesmen were starved into submission, is but one instance of severe ethnic antagonisms within these struggling new nations.[4] By no means all instances of black discrimination against other black tribal or ethnic groups can be attributed to colonialism, however.

—An unknown but substantial number of illegal immigrants enter the United States from Mexico each day. Many are leaving their home communities as a result of overpopulation, unemployment, and low economic productivity, but they are also enticed to the United States by American agricultural interests and other big employers who find it convenient to rely on their cheap labor. Many are "used" as seasonal labor and then sent home when this labor is no longer needed.[5]

—In Northern Ireland there has been a prolonged civil war between Protestants and Catholics. For all practical purposes these two groups are racially identical, and outsiders would consider them only marginally distinct ethnically. Yet the hatred between them is in many respects far greater than that between blacks and whites in the United States.

—The unemployment rate among black Americans has been approximately double that among whites for three decades. Blacks and whites are almost totally segregated from each other residentially, with blacks occupying our central cities in steadily increasing numbers. Yet for the past decade virtually no governmental policies of any magnitude have been addressed to these facts.

A list of facts such as these may tend to lead a person to cynicism rather than action. Of course there are no simple explanations or solutions to racial and ethnic discrimination, as should be obvious to anyone with even a superficial knowledge of world history. There do, however, tend to be two rather different kinds of explanations that have recurred among social analysts, beginning with the early Greek philosophers. The first views the matter in terms of basic imperfections in the "human natures" of individual people. These include the overwhelming force of self-interest, the need to find scapegoats for frustrations, individual status seeking, the tendency to be fearful or suspicious of those who differ from ourselves, and the virtual impossibility of expanding the boundaries of empathy or altruism to include more than a tiny fraction of other human beings.

The second explanation sees the problem primarily in terms of faulty human institutions that, at least in principle, are correctable. The reasons for most racial or ethnic inequality, according to some scholars, can be explained by the needs of a capitalistic system that at one stage requires cheap labor and at another leads to the virtual neglect of superfluous individuals whose labor is no longer needed. According to this view, the end of capitalism will imply the end of so-called "institutional racism." Others point to the suppression of dissent in socialist dictatorships and to the anti-Jewish policies of the government of the Soviet Union or its many attempts to suppress Georgian, Ukranian, and other nationalistic movements.

Although clearly some synthesis of these two contrasting orientations is needed—not to imply that most scholars adhere to either extreme position—it is all too tempting to create a wishy-washy synthesis that recognizes the partial validity of almost every possible explanation, without assessing the relative importance of the many factors that may be operating in each instance. Basically, what we need are methodological tools for measuring and assessing the *quantitative* impact of each type of variable. We also must learn to ask the following question: "Admitting that each of these variables has some impact, under what *conditions* will this or that kind of factor be most important, and under what conditions may certain other variables be safely ignored?" We must also anticipate that adequate theoretical explanations will have to be complex and involve multiple causes.

THE CONTENT OF THE FIELD

As is true of nearly all fields within the social sciences, there are no truly clearcut boundaries to the area of race and ethnic relations. Rather, it tends to form a set of special cases within the more general study of *intergroup processes*. For example, international relations is another field that studies the interactions between special types of groups, namely nation-states. For the most part, the field of racial and ethnic relations is concerned with patterns that occur *within* such nation-states and that usually involve a single dominant group and one or more subordinate groups, which may or may not be numerical minorities. But the field also spills over into a concern with colonialism and, therefore, the control of subordinate peoples by foreign powers. Thus, even the line between international relations and the field of racial and ethnic relations cannot be drawn too sharply.

Part of the definitional problem arises from the fact that neither races nor ethnic groups have clear-cut boundaries. The concept *race* in principle refers to biological characteristics, such as skin color, physical build, body hair, and skull measurements. In contrast, *ethnicity* refers to cultural characteristics of diverse types. Ethnic groups are those that can be distinguished on the basis of language, religion, kinship organization, dress and mannerisms, or almost any cultural characteristics deemed relevant to the actors concerned. We all recognize the existence both of racial differences and of crucial cultural distinctions that serve to set groups apart from one another. If one attempts to define such groups in terms of strictly *objective* characteristics, such as skin color, one immediately discovers that most such characteristics vary by degree and that the extent of biological intermixture is by now so great, except in the cases of a few very isolated tribes, that sharp racial delineations simply cannot be drawn. In fact, some cultural factors, such as language and religion, serve as more clear-cut distinguishing characteristics than purely racial ones.

Virtually all social scientists now agree that it is preferable to delineate racial and ethnic groups on the basis of how people are defined subjectively. The case for doing so can be well illustrated by comparing concepts of "race" in the United States and Brazil. In the United States a "black" is anyone whose biological mother or father is black. (Note that only one biological parent need be black.) Theoretically, this definition may be pushed back any number of generations, defining someone as "black" on the basis of, for example, a single black great-grandparent (though with the proviso that an extremely light-skinned "black" may successfully "pass" for white). Let us consider a hypothetical example of a boy whose father has 100-percent white ancestry and whose mother was born of a black woman and white man. This boy would have 75-percent white ancestry, but, because his mother would be socially defined as black, he too would be considered a member of this race. This pattern of categorizing offspring as belonging to the group of whichever parent has the lower status is, obviously, a mechanism for preserving a sharp dichotomy between the two groups. Everyone is clearly placed, and racial intermarriage does not permit upward mobility for one's offspring if one belongs to the lower-status group.

Contrast this situation with another in which the offspring of a black and white union would be placed in an intermediate group. Such situations have occurred, for example, where there has been a small, racially distinct, elite group—consisting of officials, soldiers, mining supervisors, plantation managers, and so forth—that contains only a very small proportion of women. A number of sexual unions between *super*ordinate-group males and *sub*ordinate females have then taken place. Where the resulting mixed-blood population has been needed to fill important occupational roles as middlemen, petty officials, or merchants, we find that a third distinct group emerges and that in many ways these persons of mixed ancestry serve as intermediaries and become marginal to both cultures. This occurrence has, in fact, been widespread throughout the world, and we shall have occasion in later chapters to compare the situation of mixed-blood populations to that of other types of minorities.

Consider what may happen if the mixing occurs rather extensively for three or four generations or if there are several different racial or ethnic groups that marry in complex combinations. In Brazil there was extensive and prolonged sexual contact between white masters and black female slaves, many of whose children were then set free. Over several generations this will obviously produce a situation in which skin color (or other racial characteristics) vary considerably by degree, and where a sharp dichotomy between black and white is no longer feasible. Thus in Brazil, which contains a considerable number of racially "black" citizens, there is no sharp dichotomy between the "races" of the form that presently exists within the United States. Instead, a person's color is considered along a *continuum*. Whiteness is favored, as is high income, but there are no distinct racial groups with clearcut boundaries.[6] The Brazilian situation, of course, differs from that of the American in a number of other important respects that may also account for the difference in social definitions. The important point is that the ultimate result has been quite different in the two settings.

The notion of "ethnic group" is equally elusive. It generally refers to groups or even categories of persons who are set apart—and who consider *themselves* as set apart—on the grounds of some set of cultural factors. Sometimes these cultural factors are both readily identifiable and crucial in terms of occupation, life style, and mode of interaction with outsiders. Language is perhaps the most obvious such characteristic. French Canadians are not only identifiable according to primary language, but they are also obviously handicapped in any situation in which English is the language of communication. Religion is another obvious cultural identifier with multiple consequences, depending upon the rituals and beliefs that accompany one's religious identification. Sometimes these may include distinctive dress patterns, ritual behaviors, or restrictions on occupational choice, food intake, work days, or the roles that may be played by married and unmarried women.

In other instances, however, an ethnic group may be defined in terms of cultural features that seem minor to outside observers but that are deliberately emphasized to set a group apart from its neighbors—small religious differences, a dialect, a particular style of clothing, or almost any other cluster of characteristics. Thus ethnic groups, like racial ones, can be considered to vary by degree. More accurately, perhaps, the *boundaries* between ethnic groups may be distinct and clearly understood by all parties, or they may be fuzzy and a matter of self-identification. One of the important theoretical and practical questions confronting the student of ethnic groups is that of how and why these boundaries are either maintained or changed.[7] Why do some American Indian tribes remain intact whereas many others have simply disappeared? To what extent are white ethnic groups, such as Italian-Americans, Polish-Americans, or Irish-Americans, still to be considered as "legitimate" ethnic groups? Are white Anglo-Saxon Protestants an ethnic group?

Therefore, when we talk about racial or ethnic "groups" we must recognize that in many instances we are really talking more about categories of persons than true groups. Thus we are faced with a further ambiguity. Sometimes we may be referring to intergroup relationships, but on other occasions the behaviors in question are more adequately described as *patterned individual actions*. That is, they are individual decisions motivated by common interests. If white city residents move to the suburbs in the face of a black "invasion," we do not imagine that this is due to a coordinated effort on the part of either the white or the black actors. Therefore, on some occasions we will be dealing with individual behaviors and relationships between individual members of different groups, whereas on others it makes more sense to think of intergroup relations among reasonably coordinated racial or ethnic groups.

The phrase "racial and ethnic groups" is cumbersome and, as we go on, will be increasingly replaced with the single word "minorities" whenever a generic term is intended. Many texts use the term "minorities" in this same sense, though it may also be used more inclusively to refer to any group facing discrimination. For example, one can refer to women, to homosexuals, or even to occupational groups (such as teachers) as minorities. This is in recognition that categories of persons other than those set apart by racial and/or cultural distinctions may face discriminatory actions and may even organize themselves and demand legal protection as minorities. (A recent case in point is that of handicapped persons.) It should be understood in this book, however, that the term "minority" will be restricted to racial and ethnic groups unless specifically noted to the contrary.

There is one more problem with the term "minority" that can be dispensed with rather briefly. The term does *not* necessarily refer to a numerical minority, but rather to a group of individuals who are in subordinate positions. For example, in some American communities blacks or Chicanos may be in a numerical majority, just as blacks constitute such a majority in South Africa. It is conventional within the field to refer to such groups as "minorities," recognizing that the relative size of a minority may itself be an important variable that helps to explain how they are treated.

Our focus will be on the *relationships* between ethnic or racial groups or their individual members. It is important to emphasize this because much of the literature in this general area focuses on specific *minorities*—their characteristics, problems, and responses—rather than on the relationship *between* groups. Persons who are members of a specific minority will obviously have a special interest in their own unique history, descriptions of existing community patterns, the nature of their institutions and leadership, and so forth.

Any serious student of race and ethnic relations will need to study the literatures on several such minorities, as case studies. But there are literally hundreds of distinct racial and ethnic minorities throughout the world, to say nothing of those that have existed in the past. For the student of racial and ethnic relations, these minorities (and their dealings with dominant groups) constitute the data from which important general principles can be inferred, with a view to yielding insights about future situations that have not yet occurred.

This distinction between an interest in specific minorities, as case studies, and the effort to establish general principles applicable to a much larger variety of intergroup situations illustrates the very different perspectives of the historian, on the one hand, and the sociologist, on the other. Therefore it is advisable to say more about it in the context of this book. Persons who are ego-involved in a situation, as members of a racial or ethnic minority inevitably must be, may be tempted to see their own problems as unique. "No minority has ever been treated as badly as we have!" "None has our unique combinations of problems!" "No one else can completely understand us!" The latter two statements will be partly correct, though the former will most certainly not. Although perfectly understandable, many sociologists would argue that such thinking is unfortunate, for several reasons.

First, it inhibits cooperation and mutual understanding among racial and ethnic groups, each of which is telling its own unique horror story. Second, and perhaps more important, it tends to block efforts to search for similarities and differences that lead to important *theoretical* insights that can be applied to other situations. Take, for example, the case of blacks and slavery. It is true that no members of other American minorities were forceably removed from Africa, shipped to a totally strange setting, sold into slavery, separated from practically all their friends and relatives, and then literally owned outright as a piece of personal property. Likewise, American Indian experiences are also unique. Chicanos, who usually share some Indian ancestry, can also point to a distinct history. Furthermore, it is highly unlikely that these histories will ever be even partially repeated in the future. As true as that statement may be, however, we may learn from history only if we can formulate general propositions that may then be tested and evaluated on other sets of data, including other settings throughout the world, both past and present.

To believe that one particular minority has been abused and discriminated against more than others is to lose the opportunity to compare and learn from the histories of other minorities. For example, under what *conditions* is slavery more likely to arise than another form of economic arrangement? All three of the above-mentioned minorities have had to supply their labor for what almost anyone would consider an "unfair" rate of exchange. Blacks were brought to the New World precisely because most American Indian tribes were not sufficiently numerous to be used as cheap labor. In areas of Mexico and Central America, however, Indians were also subjected to a similar form of economic treatment. It was not the institution of slavery, per se, but rather a form of tribute extracted by Spanish managers of so-called "encomiendas." In the case of many Chicanos who have immigrated across the Mexican border, the pattern has taken the form of "free" migratory farm labor paid at much lower wages than those of nonmigrant farm labor and reinforced by the fear that illegal immigrants could, at any time, be rounded up and sent back home. Because of the labor surplus encouraged by this process, there has been no need for the actual ownership of the worker as slave property. Indeed, the situations that black, Indian, and Chicano laborers faced were unique; but they also were similar in many respects. Hence, the need is to *compare* such minority situations and then to extract from them a set of variables (factors that vary by degree) and to study how these are interrelated. Each particular minority and setting can then be characterized by a unique combination of scores or values on these variables, just as every person has a unique combination of age, height, shade of skin color, or occupation.

The ultimate goal of the process is to build theories complex enough to make useful predictions about events that have either not yet occurred or about which we do not have the relevant empirical information. In constructing and fine-tuning these theories, however, we must rely as much as possible on specific historical data. Needless to say, much of the information we would ideally like to have is lost in history.

Since most readers will be much more familiar with American minorities—and in particular with blacks, Hispanics, Asian-Americans, and American Indians, groups that are *currently* being referred to as "legitimate" minorities—I shall follow the practice of illustrating points primarily in terms of these particular minorities. Whenever contrasting or similar situations pertaining to other parts of the world seem relevant, however, I shall not hesitate to bring them in. The principal aim is to provide the reader with a rather general roadmap of the field, rather than a large number of concrete illustrations. Once this roadmap has been studied, it will then make sense to begin intensive study of particular minorities and their relationships with dominant groups, always paying attention to the settings and constraints under which both groups are operating.

NOTES

1. See, for instance, Eric Williams, *Capitalism and Slavery* (New York: Capricorn Books, 1966).

2. Among the many books that have been written on this subject see especially Carey McWilliams, *Prejudice: Japanese-Americans* (Boston: Little, Brown, 1945); Alexander Leighton, *The Governing of Men* (Princeton, N.J.: Princeton University Press, 1945); and Dorothy S. Thomas and Richard S. Nishomoto, *The Spoilage* (Berkeley: University of California Press, 1946).

3. See H. M. Blalock, *Toward a Theory of Minority-Group Relations* (New York: Wiley, 1967), pp. 79–84; and Lea E. Williams, *Southeast Asia: A History* (New York: Oxford University Press, 1976).

4. See E. K. Francis, *Interethnic Relations: An Essay in Sociological Theory* (New York: Elsevier, 1976), pp. 318–24.

5. This migrant labor problem will be discussed in chapter 3.

6. A similar blending of races has occurred in Hawaii, with the result that our fiftieth state enjoys the reputation of having low levels of prejudice and discrimination in spite of its very high minority percentage.

7. See Fredrik Barth (ed.), *Ethnic Groups and Boundaries* (Boston: Little, Brown, 1969).

CHAPTER 2
THEORIES
OF INDIVIDUAL
PREJUDICE

As noted in the introduction, the subject of race and ethnic relations cuts across a number of fields. Probably the largest bodies of literature exist within psychology and sociology, but political scientists, economists, and geographers have also given increasing attention to the subject. Likewise, historians and anthropologists have provided diverse factual materials that need to be incorporated into any reasonably inclusive explanation.

Such an explanatory system must include two very different levels of analysis. The first, which we shall refer to as the *micro-level* is oriented toward accounting for the behaviors of individual persons. People make decisions that are subject to constraints, which vary with the circumstances. Also, because they have multiple goals that cannot all be satisfied simultaneously, they must make conscious or unconscious decisions, choosing among alternative means according to some judgment as to their relative efficiency, cost, or probability of success. These choices often affect other persons, including minorities. Furthermore, the choices individuals make are influenced by the beliefs they hold about these other persons. Some of these beliefs may be accurate, whereas others may be highly distorted. At this micro-level, then, our focus is primarily on the individual and his or her responses to stimuli of various types. This orientation is basically psychological and social psychological.

The second explanatory system, which we shall refer to as the *macro-level*, stresses macro-comparative studies and variables that pertain primarily to the group, such as the following factors: the nature of a society's economy and division of labor; a society's political structure and the normative supports for this structure; the extent of inequality that exists among various strata; religious and linguistic differences that have existed historically; the degree to which groups are geographically segregated; and many other similar factors.

It would be to our advantage if micro theories about individual behaviors were closely linked to those that refer to macro processes at the group level. Certainly they should not be mutually inconsistent or incompatible. Yet we find a number of scholars, approaching these questions from both directions, who believe either that the theories are in some sense opposed or, at the very least, that only one or the other need be taken seriously. The focus of attention in the remaining chapters will be on relatively more macro-oriented issues, but with the recognition that macro-level explanations must always be built upon micro-level assumptions about individual behaviors and motivations.[1]

In these later chapters the reader will discover that an emphasis is placed on behavior oriented to the achievement of rather specific objectives, such as status or economic goals. To complement this orientation, therefore, we must pay attention to a rather extensive body of literature that stresses not only the subconscious and emotional aspects of human behavior but also that is intended to explain some of the most extreme forms of aggression known to mankind. Any reasonably complete explanation of minority relations must cope with such extreme phenomena, as well as those that are more amenable to "rationalistic" economic types of analyses.

PSYCHODYNAMIC THEORIES OF AGGRESSION

Antisemitism has had a long and brutal history in Europe. For instance, during medieval times Jews were blamed for unexplained crises such as the Bubonic plague, which decimated much of Europe during the fourteenth century. By the time of the midnineteenth century, however, it appeared as though many West European Jews would become absorbed into the economies of each of the separate nation-states that vied with each other for economic and political power. About this time, however, the writings of several racist scholars, notably Arthur de Gobineau and Stewart Chamberlain, began to attract the attention of certain elite groups who, for one reason or another, found they could turn them to their own advantage.[2] In particular, antisemitism was manipulated by Bismarck and other German leaders fully a half-century prior to the rise of Adolph Hitler.[3] Whenever these elites found it to their interest to divert protest movements, such as those of organized labor, they did not hesitate to invoke antisemitism.

Nevertheless, despite such virulent antisemitism Jewish intermarriage with German Gentiles was widespread by the time of Hitler's rise to power. This fact made it difficult to recognize persons with mixed Jewish-Gentile ancestry. But by the same token it also made it easier to convince a willing public that "German blood" was being polluted and that Jews were to blame for all sorts of things: the loss of World War I, much of the humiliation and disorganization that followed Germany's defeat, uncontrolled inflation, and even the Great Depression of the 1930's.

The extreme nature of Hitler's antisemitic policies was not fully realized until after the war, when captured films documented the systematic slaughter of some six million Jews. It also became evident that thousands of German citizens *actively* participated in these murders, apparently gaining "satisfaction" in carrying out Hitler's plans. There are tales of persons who made lampshades of human flesh, engaged in sadistic rapes, conducted numerous "scientific" experiments involving unbelievable barbarities, and much more. How can these behaviors be explained? How could millions of highly educated German people enthusiastically endorse and actually cooperate with such a leader? Why did they eagerly take part in earlier riots against Jewish citizens, many of whom had been their own friends? Why did they remain conveniently ignorant of the Nazi death chambers? Can all of this be explained in terms of blind obedience or simple fear?

Recognizing that the rise of Hitler and his policy of mass genocide were but extreme instances of forms of racial and ethnic hatred, and noting that our own American history contained many similar instances of highly sadistic forms of violence, a number of scholars set out to explain these phenomena in works that were published during the 1940s and 1950s. Perhaps the most important works in this field were *The Authoritarian Personality*, by T. W. Adorno and others, and the research of Dollard, Miller, and others on theories of frustration and aggression.[4] As with similar works, these relied heavily on ideas proposed by psychoanalysts, both Freudian and Neofreudian, who emphasized the importance of repressed impulses and subconscious processes rooted deeply in the personality. In essence they were an effort to make sense of the very massive breakdown in what had been taken to be the epitomy of a highly "rationalistic" social system, namely, Germany in the first half of the twentieth century.

The authors of *The Authoritarian Personality* organized their psychodynamic theory around the concept of "authoritarianism," which they argued consisted of a number of interrelated dimensions. The authoritarian personality, they held, is one who both eagerly submits to some form of rigid authority and also aggresses against those who reject this authority or who are defined as "outsiders." Those who score high on what was referred to as the "F-Scale," which is used to measure authoritarianism, are persons who not only display these dual tendencies to defer to authority and to aggress against outsiders but who also tend to see the world in terms of power and toughness, who are highly suspicious that conspiracies are being hatched by their enemies, and who tend to think in dichotomized terms. They use rigid categories that divide others into the strong and the weak and into the good and the evil, and they also tend to have rigid and inflexible thought processes.

All of these authoritarian characteristics encourage aggression against those who are defined as being in the "wrong" category—Jews in the case of the Nazis, blacks in the case of the Southern lynch mob, or "the enemy" in the case of a war. These characteristics also make possible submission to authoritarian leadership without questioning orders. There are obvious parallels, of course, to what pacificists see as the stereotypical "blind" military mind—the kind of person who can unthinkingly murder enemy civilians, as occurred at My Lai during the Vietnam War.

Hundreds of studies have now been conducted replicating the fact that the F-Scale correlates positively with antisemitism, anti-black prejudice, hostility toward out-groups of many kinds, and with various kinds of socialization experiences encouraging strict obedience, the rigid adherence to fundamentalist religious beliefs, and a general inflexibility in coping with new situations. Virtually all of these studies have shown an inverse relationship between authoritarianism and extent of education. It has been argued that, in part, the last factor may be a result of question wording: a number of questions used in the F-Scale are unlikely to be endorsed by educated persons, and all items are worded in such a fashion that a "yes" answer indicates high authoritarianism. Therefore persons who tend to agree with questions, regardless of their content, will automatically score high. Even so, it seems clear that authoritarianism is a reasonable predictor of prejudice, as well as many other forms of rejection of out-groups, of suspiciousness toward others, and of general alienation from many democratic institutions. This finding is not restricted to majority populations. For example, it holds for blacks as well as whites.

The F-Scale has been criticized on a number of counts and is currently used much less frequently in social psychological research.[5] One criticism is that the concept, as well as the scale itself, is far too broad and multidimensional. In effect, it contains a little bit of everything and therefore correlates moderately (usually between .3 and .5) with a large number of variables.[6] On theoretical grounds perhaps the most constructive criticism is that the concept confuses a very general type of thinking involving rigidity, a lack of openness to new ideas, and a tendency to dichotomize, on the one hand, with political conservatism, on the other. That is, it is basically concerned with right-wing authoritarianism rather than with left-wing authoritarianism, with which it also has much in common.[7] Thus extreme Marxists may be equally rigid, aggressive toward those who reject Marxist dogma, and submissive to authority. Yet they may not share many of the other ideas linked with the original "authoritarianism" of Adorno and his associates, and they may not be prejudiced toward minorities. Rokeach, in a series of later investigations, has stressed that the essential characteristic of both right-wing and left-wing authoritarianism is an unwillingness to modify one's beliefs in the face of contrary evidence.[8] Rokeach also argues that prejudice may be much more closely linked to the phenomenon of rejecting persons who believe differently from ourselves, rather than to racial or ethnic memberships per se.

At about the same time that studies of authoritarianism among individuals were highly popular among social psychologists, others were writing along similar lines but on a more macro-oriented level. One of the most influential writers approaching the subject from a psychoanalytic, Neofreudian perspective was Erich Fromm, whose *Escape from Freedom* stressed the theme that Western man has gained a new type of freedom from traditional authority that is at the same time producing intolerable strains for many individuals.[9] Lacking an inner sense of direction and genuine self-love, these persons find it necessary to escape from their newly gained freedom from tradition by various mechanisms, one of which is to believe rigidly in the doctrines and programs of some authoritarian figure. Sometimes this may be a religious authority, such as Martin Luther, or it may be a political leader with a highly simplistic program that promises security in return for unquestioned loyalty. Obviously, Fromm's thesis constitutes a macro-level argument that is highly compatible with the micro-level authoritarian-personality approach.

A third psychodynamic orientation that will play a more important role in our later discussions is that of the frustration-aggression mechanism. As originally formulated by Dollard and Miller, the theory contained the assumption that frustration—the blockage of a goal—is *always* followed by some form of aggression, defined as behavior whose purpose is the injury of some party.[10] This aggression need not always be directed toward the actual source of frustration, however. Indeed, in many instances the causes of the goal blockage may be highly complex, may not be due to any single human agent, or may be very poorly understood by the actor concerned. Or the cause of goal blockage may be a specific but very powerful force and thus capable of inflicting severe punishment for aggression. Therefore, the aggression may be *displaced* onto a different target. It may also be very subtle or indirect, and perhaps delayed as well.

Given this possibility of displacement and delay, and, therefore, the difficulty of establishing a direct connection between a given frustration and a particular act of aggression, the assumption of an inevitable connection between frustration and aggression becomes exceedingly difficult to test empirically. By allowing for long enough delays, very subtle forms of aggression, and displacement onto almost any target, it becomes possible to argue that almost *any* later act constitutes a form of aggression caused by any particular frustration.

Nevertheless the theory seems highly plausible. Problematic, however, is the question of how one makes specific predictions as to the choice of target, given displacement, as well as the forms that the aggression may take. One theory suggests that the target will be "similar" to the source of frustration, or at least that it will symbolize it in some way. Similarity is also a vague term, however. More plausible, perhaps, is the argument that the target, where displacement occurs, will tend to have a number of desirable characteristics, including visibility, availability, and vulnerability.[11]

Aggression against such a target will be likely if it is also *instrumental* toward some other goal. A highly visible but unprotected minority may thus constitute an ideal scapegoat, especially if it has something that the aggressor wants. Thus white European aggression against helpless Indians in possession of valued land served not only as an outlet for aggression but also made it possible to secure that land. Aggression against Japanese-Americans after Pearl Harbor resulted in their removal to "relocation centers" and their loss of land, property, and jobs. Aggression against Asian residents in black-dominated Uganda led to their expulsion and the takeover of profitable business operations.

Thus both the frustration-aggression hypothesis and the authoritarian-personality hypothesis (that individuals with authoritarian personalities will tend to reject and aggress against outsiders) are reasonably well established empirically but are also rather slippery with respect to their ability to make specific predictions. In particular, they seem much more adequate in explaining the *intensity* of behaviors directed toward a given minority than in explaining why a particular minority, or other target, has been selected in the first place.

Once Hitler had designated Jews as a target, and once the German people had found it convenient to believe Hitler's attacks on this specific minority, we can begin to understand—though perhaps never fully comprehend—why they may have acted so aggressively against the Jewish people. Germany had experienced severe frustration and humiliation following World War I. Combined with postwar frustration were uncertainties produced by runaway inflation, a major depression, and what appeared to be a floundering leadership. We can perhaps imagine how the intense persecution of Jews came about, once Hitler's program became accepted and gave every appearance of actually working. Then, as defeat seemed near, as German cities themselves began to suffer severe war damage, and as casualties mounted, we can begin to understand how a sufficient number of Hitler's loyal followers were willing to cooperate fully in the "final solution" (extermination) for Jews. A highly rationalistic analysis in terms of Gentile self-interest or actual competition with Jews would hardly suffice as an adequate explanation for these extreme behaviors.

Even in situations in which there is obvious competition between racial or ethnic groups, and where there is no need to invoke psychodynamic explanations, there will inevitably be important individual differences within all groups. For instance, if we are to give credence to historical accounts of conflicts between American Indians and whites, there were a number of white generals who had considerable respect for their enemies, who protected them from the excesses of their own troops, and who in good faith attempted to negotiate what they considered to be just treaties with the Indians.[12] The fact that virtually all these treaties were later violated does not mean that these efforts were hypocritical or insincere; they merely may have been made by men who failed to anticipate later developments or the greed of many of their fellow whites. In short, there *are* personality differences within any group which will influence behaviors over and beyond the factors that will later become the focus of our attention.

SUBJECTIVE EXPECTED UTILITIES
(SEU) AND CHOICE BEHAVIOR

Since human actors obviously have a wide range of choices from among alternative behaviors, and since racial and ethnic minorities need not be relevant to these choices, we must consider the factors that affect how people choose their behaviors. Sometimes choices will be subject to severe constraints. For instance, in a predominantly agricultural economy arable land is an absolutely essential resource. If the best land is occupied by a relatively powerless indigenous group, as for example, American Indians, one can expect a conflict to occur over this scarce resource if a stronger outside group enters the picture, with the result that the weaker group will either be exterminated or forced onto less desirable land. In other instances, however, choices are much less restricted; then, matters of personal preference, of local attitudes and prejudices, or of convenience may be most important in determining behavior. This often is the case, for example, with respect to choices in selecting from among more familiar, modern-day alternatives, such as residential neighborhoods, social clubs, and friendship cliques. Here, choices are subject to wide, subjective influences.

Goals, values, and beliefs—subjective states—in turn, will be influenced by external factors impinging on individuals. Whenever one deals with these subjective variables, however, there is a danger of allowing the theory to become far too complex and confusing to permit definitive predictions. To allow for the operation of subjective factors while still keeping the argument relatively simple, we shall use an approach developed by economists and psychologists oriented to decision theories. We emphasize, however, that this is not the only possible orientation and that it is weakest precisely where the psychodynamic theories are strongest, namely in dealing with subconscious, deep-seated personality needs that result in highly emotional states and extreme forms of behavior.

We assume that most if not all stimuli that impinge on the human actor operate through one or both of two kinds of variables: utilities and subjective probabilities. *Utilities* refer to the subjective values attached to goals or outcomes, as for example that of earning a certain income, winning a particular marriage partner, becoming president of the United States, or avoiding conflict. Many outcomes are complex in the sense that they may satisfy multiple goals or may satisfy one goal but frustrate another. It is perhaps simplest, then, to think in terms of specific goals and to assume that actors attach subjective values, or utilities, to each of these goals. Any given outcome can then be evaluated in terms of the goals it does or does not satisfy.

If a given behavior always resulted in the desired outcome, it would be rather simple to make a rough calculation of its expected total utility by simply adding the utilities of each of the goals that would be satisfied by that behavior. But uncertainty will almost always enter the picture, so that each actor needs to make a rough assessment of the probability that the outcome will occur, given the behavior, as compared with its likelihood if the behavior does not take place. This is the process of attaching *subjective probabilities*, referred to above, to evaluate possible routes to desired goals. Such subjective probabilities will undoubtedly be influenced by past experience as well as many other factors. Perceptual distortions may enter. For example, there is some experimental evidence to show that subjective probabilities may be influenced by utilities, with highly valued goals tending to be associated with overly high subjective probabilities.[13] This might be thought of as the "wishful thinking" bias; that is, we tend to believe that good things will happen more frequently than is actually the case. Also, people tend to overestimate very small probabilities and underestimate very high ones.

Subjective probabilities are also influenced by what we may refer to as actors' "working causal theories." That is, people tend to believe that certain actions will result in particular outcomes because they assume the existence of causal connections between variables. Thus I may believe that if I work hard and get good grades in school, this will assure me of a good job. Or, if I am a minority member, I may believe that no matter what I do my chances for success are very slim. These beliefs may or may not turn out to be correct. The essential point is that these subjective probabilities will influence our behavior, which cannot be understood by outside observers unless they somehow take them into consideration.

How are these subjective probabilities and utilities fitted together or combined? It is a fundamental assumption in subjective expected utility (SEU) theory that they are *multiplied*. In the simplest case where there is only one goal and one possible way of achieving it, the behavior level would be proportional to the product of the subjective probability p multiplied by the utility U. In more complicated cases these products of p and U would need to be added over the total number of goals being considered.[14]

Obviously, no real human beings ever conform to this idealized model of behavior. In the first place, because no one can consider all possible alternative behaviors that might achieve a goal, each person must settle on a much smaller set. Some alternatives will never even occur to the individual. Others will have such low subjective probabilities associated with them that, in effect, these will be mentally given a probability of zero, with the result that the behavior will be ruled out completely. Likewise, no one can place a precise "numerical" value on a utility, though we must assume that goals can be *ordered* with respect to these subjective values. Nor can one come up with more than rather crude subjective probabilities, such as "near zero," "about 50-50," or "almost certain." Nevertheless we assume that actors do make some such rather crude calculations, many of which will not be fully conscious.

From this rather simplified formulation we can see that a behavior will not be enacted for *either* of the following two reasons: (1) if it involves an extremely small subjective probability, or (2) if the utility is near zero, regardless of the subjective probability. Thus a rat in a maze will not try to attain food if, through repeated trials, it learns that the behavior virtually never yields the food. Nor will it try to get to the food if it is not hungry, that is, if it is satiated so that the utility for food is for all practical purposes zero. In the case of minority individuals, we often expect to find high utilities associated with very low subjective probabilities. In other words, minority members may want something very much but may have come to realize that they can never achieve it, regardless of their behaviors. From the point of view of an outside observer, if we observe that a behavior is not taking place, we will not know whether this is due to a very small utility, a very low subjective probability, or possibly both. It would be erroneous, for example, to assume that minorities are "satisfied" (that is, do not want something) when, in fact, they may merely be discouraged or fatalistic.

In most real-world situations there will be multiple goals; there will also be complex outcomes that satisfy these goals to varying degrees, as well as many different means (behaviors) to achieve them, each involving a different subjective probability. Clearly, a "rational" actor who attempted to carry out the precise mental calculations that seem to be implied by the SEU decision-making theory could very quickly become immobilized. Simplifications of one type or another, therefore, will be absolutely essential. Here is where ideologies, simplified sterotypes about other people, and normative group pressures will enter the picture. For example, someone may rule out a whole set of alternatives because they have been defined as ethically wrong. In effect, if he or she were to use these means the resulting expected punishment (including guilt) might reduce the subjective expected utility (SEU) for this alternative to a very low value. Other alternatives may be ruled out because one believes in extremely simplified explanations that discount the possibility of these alternatives ever being effective. Still others may never even be considered because no one has ever suggested them.

Therefore, if the social scientist is to be in a position to predict behavior in advance of its occurring, he or she must know something about not only the relative importance of different goals to the individuals (that is, their utilities) but also the nature of the simplifying assumptions they are likely to make. This is obviously a difficult task. Fortunately, in the field of minority relations we need not be concerned with *all* goals actors may have but merely a small subset of these. In particular, when we are concerned with the behaviors of majority or dominant-group individuals, we may focus on those behaviors that bear directly on minorities. For instance, dominant-group members may attempt to use the minority as a means to an end (for example, through slavery to produce a very cheap labor supply), in effect entering into an exchange with the minority in which dominant-group members gain much more than they give up.

In the chapters that follow we shall be concerned with five very general types of behavior that bear directly on the nature of interactions between majority-group and minority-group members. We note them here only in passing to suggest their bearing on the present discussion. They are: (1) "exploitive" relationships, in which one party uses another as a means to achieve its own objectives and extracts what is perceived to be an unfair exchange rate between them;

(2) competitive behavior, where the two parties are vying for the same scarce objectives; (3) aggression, where one party is attempting to injure the other, but not necessarily as a means to another objective; (4) discrimination, or the differential treatment of minority-group and dominant-group members; and (5) avoidance behavior, through which one or both groups attempt to reduce the extent of contact with the other.

Once we have covered all five types of behaviors (from the viewpoint of both actors and "reactors"), we will have covered most of the topics that are ordinarily considered within the field of race and ethnic relations. In each case, however, we shall also need to discuss the social conditions that affect each type of behavior, thus forcing us to consider macro-level phenomena, where groups are the focus of attention.

COGNITIVE THEORIES OF PREJUDICE

Two other theories explaining prejudice and discrimination, namely, those that stress cognitive processes and conformity to group norms, can be rather directly linked to the SEU formulation. Here we shall briefly outline the nature of these theories, which we can then call upon later in dealing with the five general behavior types previously mentioned.

Prejudice almost always involves a cognitive dimension along with feelings and preferences. The prejudiced person develops *stereotypes,* or simplified beliefs, about minorities; although partly based on fact, more often than not these stereotypes are rigidly held and resistant to contrary factual evidence. To some extent, of course, *all* thinking must involve the use of oversimplified categories. Young children learn that barking dogs are to be avoided, that strangers are not to be trusted, that somewhat older children are likely to look down upon them, and that—in general—things that look alike tend to behave similarly. From here it is but a small step to generalizing about the characteristics of persons who look alike racially, who dress in distinctive ways, who speak with accents, or who are simply labeled as outsiders.

As Gordon Allport has pointed out, the formation of simplified stereotypes is functional in the sense that it facilitates our decision-making processes.[15] Furthermore, we tend to make only those distinctions that seem directly relevant and useful to us. If we can classify all persons of a given type as alike, we will tend to maintain these beliefs unless and until it is to our advantage to change them. This is merely a special case of the principle of "least effort," namely, that modifying our thought processes is always costly to some degree.[16] Thus stereotyping and generalizing are natural phenomena.

Clearly, however, some people are more resistant to changing their beliefs than others. In part, this may be due to personality differences including the kinds of rigidities analyzed in psychodynamic theories of prejudice. It may also be due to social pressures. If there are no real incentives to change one's beliefs, why should one do so? This is especially true if those persons with whom one interacts also tend to believe the same things and if they continually reinforce whatever negative stereotypes one may have? This tendency to hold on to rigid stereotypes seems closely linked to the tendency to dichotomize and to think in terms of extreme contrasts such as good and evil, beautiful and ugly, or powerful and submissive.

Persons obviously differ with respect to their cognitive skills or their ability to see through, and therefore modify, very simple generalizations based on rigid categorization. Thus one would expect that stereotyping or cognitive forms of prejudice will be functions of one's level of education and perhaps one's "native intelligence," assuming the latter could be accurately measured. Indeed, most studies of prejudice that use the survey format, where the cognitive dimension is most likely to be tapped, show that prejudice is practically always negatively associated with level of education. This is, in fact, the one truly consistent finding of surveys conducted since World War II. Quinley and Glock, authors of *Anti-Semitism in America*, after examining a host of empirical results concerning both antisemitism and anti-black prejudice, concluded that education and cognitive sophistication are by far the best predictors of these forms of prejudice.[17] They noted, however, that these conclusions might not apply to more virulent forms of prejudice, as for example the kind of antisemitism that existed for several decades in Germany prior to the rise of Hitler.

One's beliefs also can be expected to bear directly on one's subjective probabilities. Thus a white parent who believes that blacks will lower the quality of education received by his or her own children will assign a much lower subjective probability to getting a good education in an integrated school than in a segregated all-white school. Thus one's policy preferences will depend not only upon utilities but also subjective probabilities, which are directly influenced by one's beliefs. Presumably, if these beliefs about black students could be changed, so could one's assessments of subjective probabilities. For instance, busing to achieve racial balance—or other devices that assure a mixture of races within each school—would be less resisted even without a basic change in utilities for quality education.

In practice it is often very difficult to separate cognitive components of prejudice from a person's feelings and personality needs, and—as one might expect—the two components are usually found to be moderately highly intercorrelated. Given this fact, it is often difficult to rely on strictly empirical evidence to decide, definitively, whether cognitive processes predominate over feelings or emotions. Undoubtedly this also varies from one individual to the next.

Given this link between cognitive and *affective* (or feeling) components, one should not expect a given set of beliefs to hang together too consistently. Instead, the rational actor may be expected to cast about for those beliefs that are *convenient*, given his or her set of utilities. Specific minority stereotypes may, in fact, shift from time to time according to the circumstances. Allport points out that one may "fence in" a set of beliefs by periodically admitting to exceptions—the occasional black who is highly intelligent or the Jewish acquaintance who is scrupulously honest.[18] By defining such persons as exceptions, one may then proceed to condemn the vast majority of others in that social category who, presumably, are really "typical."

To identify the convenience and "rationality" of cognitive belief systems, we may ask what kinds of attributes it would be convenient to believe about two very different types of minorities that are commonly found throughout the world. The first is the lower-class, down-and-out minority that is required to perform the most menial, distasteful, and dangerous types of work. It would be convenient to believe that members of such a minority are basically inept: of low native intelligence, lazy and unambitious, unable or unwilling to plan for the future and oriented only to present pleasures, unclean and otherwise unpleasant to associate with, and in general deserving of their low status. It would also be convenient to believe that they are basically contented or even happy, childlike and appreciative of small favors, and able to get along with a much lower standard of living than members of one's own group. A few "positive" stereotypes are also convenient, if only to persuade oneself that one is not doing the minority an injustice. So they may be believed to possess certain secondary kinds of talents: a good sense of humor, unusual musical abilities, a certain humility, and so forth. If the minority is beginning to show signs of not accepting the system or of openly rebelling, however, additional stereotypes are likely to accompany these. They may be typed as dangerous, unruly, criminally inclined, surly, and unappreciative.

Now suppose we are dealing with a less common type of minority, one which is economically well off, and thus which we might wish to suppress or to deprive of its favored economic position. Of this second group it is convenient to believe that its members have gained their positions by illegitimate or shady means: through fraud, dishonest or unethical business techniques, overcharging customers, or sweatshop labor practices. Its members are also likely to be characterized as *overly* ambitious and as showing undue favoritism toward their own group. They are "pushy" and often intrude too much into others' affairs, trying too hard to climb the social ladder. They are "nouveau riche" or "gauche" in social affairs, or they are hypocritical and not to be trusted.

It would be hard not to recognize in these stereotypes commonly held beliefs about current American minorities: in the first instance, blacks and Hispanics; in the second, Jews. What may be less well known is that these very same stereotypes have been applied to other groups from around the world and over a relatively long period of time. Many immigrants to the United States—especially the Irish, Italians, Poles, and most Southern Europeans—were characterized according to the first set of beliefs. Middle-class minorities, such as the Chinese in Southeast Asia and, to a lesser extent, Japanese-Americans in the United States, have been characterized in ways almost identical to the stereotypes about Jews in Europe and the United States. This is obviously not coincidental and can be explained, in large part, by noting how convenient these beliefs are to the would-be discriminator.

Believing certain things about the nature of the *social system* that has placed minorities where they are also serves the interests of dominant-group members. If one is dealing with a lower-class minority at the bottom of the social and economic ladder, it is convenient to believe that the system is basically fair and that persons at the bottom are getting their just deserts. Presumably, then, they can legitimately raise themselves only by being better behaved: working harder, getting more education, saving their money, thinking more about the future, controlling their antisocial behaviors, taking baths, and so forth. If there are certain features of the social system that are difficult to justify, a second line of defense is to believe that these inconsistencies are inevitable, willed by God, or only very slowly changed by some vague process such as "the passage of time."

Certain belief systems work in the opposite direction, but this does not mean that they, too, cannot be conveniently modified to suit one's set of value preferences (utilities). For example, the unfairness of the "system" can be blamed entirely on members of elite groups, who are believed to be conspiring secretly to manipulate the masses. Such explanations are common among those who would like to justify the lack of cooperative action among those in similar class positions. Thus, if white and black working-class groups are in mutual conflict, this is blamed on a capitalist elite who, somehow, manipulate these groups into hostility. Presumably, under another type of economic system, such as communism, all conflicts between these groups would disappear.

The phenomenon of ethnocentrism has long been noted as characterizing a wide variety of relationships between groups, including small cliques as well as nation-states. *Ethnocentrism* refers to the belief that one's own group—its patterns of interaction and its culture—is superior to other groups. Ethnocentrism, however, may vary by degree both among individual members of a group and across groups. Historically, although many dominant groups have been highly ethnocentric toward both internal minorities and their outside neighbors, there have been a few instances where dominant groups have actually looked upon conquered minorities as culturally superior to themselves.

As a general rule, a high degree of ethnocentrism on the part of a *minority* serves the function of enabling it to perpetuate its own distinctive culture in the presence of pressures to assimilate to the dominant culture. Such ethnocentrism, however, is often resented and serves not only to set the group apart but also to help justify aggression against it during crisis periods. Nonmembers naturally interpret such highly ethnocentric beliefs as extremely oversimplified and unjustified. Further, when two or more highly ethnocentric groups are in close interaction, there automatically exist some extremely handy rationalizations for engaging in mutually antagonistic behaviors.

The essential point is that cognitive stereotypes, in all these instances, represent simplifications of a real world that is much more complex. These simplifications permit definitive actions, as well as later justifications for these actions. Since in that sense they are "rational" for the individual actor, it would be a mistake to claim that such beliefs are completely determined by noncognitive factors, such as feeling states or vested interests. But they will generally be made consistent with them, given the enormous range of possible beliefs the human mind is capable of inventing. This implies that subjective expectations are also readily distorted by these beliefs.

CONFORMITY TO GROUP NORMS

Another very common thesis among sociologists is that individuals are prejudiced and engage in discrimination primarily because they are conforming to group norms. If so, then one's explanation of these phenomena must be taken closer to the macro-level, where these norms themselves must be explained in terms of other variables. In terms of subjective expected utilities, most persons are motivated to value high status within whatever groups they select as positive reference groups.[19] Most persons also wish to avoid negative sanctions (punishments) in groups of which they are actual members. In the case of norms, regulations, or laws of any importance in these groups, conformity will generally be rewarded and deviance punished. Therefore, if these norms stress that minorities should be treated in a certain fashion, the overwhelming majority of group members will conform regardless of their personality needs or deep-seated feelings about minorities. In this sense, then, most such behaviors are "superficial" and do not need to be explained in psychodynamic terms.

This type of explanation obviously competes with the psychodynamic one, and if all the variables in each theory could be accurately measured it would then be possible to evaluate their relative explanatory power. The normative explanation places a premium on distinguishing between attitudes, which presumably depend partly on personality needs and early socialization, and actual behaviors, which need not be compatible with these beliefs and feelings.[20] Thus the highly prejudiced person may be made to conform to nondiscriminatory regulations, just as the individual with very low prejudice may elect to discriminate in order to gain status in the group. Where the norms relating to racial and ethnic groups are unequivocal and actually enforced through sanctions, this argument indeed makes a great deal of sense. It is the basic thesis of those who claim that behaviors can be drastically modified through legal actions, provided these are strictly enforced. The very rapid changes that occurred in most Southern states during the 1960s and early 1970s regarding the treatment of blacks in restaurants, hotels, parks, stores, theaters, and even as co-workers are convincing evidence that there is much to be said for this position. Certainly, deep-seated personality characteristics could not have changed so rapidly.

Individuals obviously differ with respect to how much value they attach to conforming with group norms. Furthermore, in many instances they may self-select themselves into and out of groups according to the fit between their own value preferences and those of other group members. This is one reason why it is often difficult to evaluate the two theories empirically. We often do not know whether persons are conforming in spite of their own preferences or have instead selected themselves into groups that share these preferences.

Persons also differ with respect to utilities attached to achieving *status* within the group. This is not quite the same thing as values attached to conformity, unless the norms concerned are of central importance to the group. Often norms that relate to the treatment of minorities are not of great significance in a given group, so that someone who conforms to more important norms, and who has high status, may be able to violate these lesser norms with impunity. Therefore in evaluating the normative conformity argument one always has to ask the dual questions: How important is the achievement of status in this particular group to this individual? And how important is this particular norm (relating to the minority) in this group?

Several studies conducted in the 1950s showed modest correlations—of the same order of magnitude as correlations with the F-Scale—between what was termed "status concern" or "status consciousness" and prejudice toward several minorities.[21] The thesis was that persons who were generally concerned with matters of status and position in the social hierarchy would tend to display prejudice toward minorities merely because this was "the thing to do" or because *any* association with low-status persons would lower their own status in the eyes of most majority individuals. But by the same token, if it suddenly became fashionable to favor these same minorities, these persons might be expected to display the *least* prejudice.

The normative conformity theory, while downgrading the psychodynamic orientation and stressing more surface-level factors, carries with it a disturbing implication. It suggests that if any factors began to work in the larger society to shift these norms substantially—for example, as might result from a major economic crisis or the rise of a demagogic leader—attitudes and behaviors toward minorities could also change very rapidly. There would be few if any "brakes" of the type that might be expected if, say, early socialization and deep-seated personality needs were the primary factors at work. Thus there could be major ups and downs in the treatment of minorities, according to the circumstances. This thesis, then, is highly compatible with a number of other theories that place the emphasis more directly on macro-level causes of prejudice and discrimination. To these we now turn our attention.

NOTES

1. This point of view is developed in considerably more detail in H. M. Blalock and Paul H. Wilken, *Intergroup Processes: A Micro-Macro Approach* (New York: Free Press, 1979).

2. See Louis L. Snyder, *Race: A History of Modern Ethnic Theories* (New York: Longmans, Green, 1939).

3. See Paul W. Massing, *Rehearsal for Destruction* (New York: Harper & Row,

Pub., 1949). For an alternative interpretation of the rise of antisemitism in Germany see Hannah Arendt, *The Origins of Totalitarianism* (New York: Harcourt Brace Jovanovich, Inc., 1973 edition).

4. See T. W. Adorno, et al., *The Authoritarian Personality* (New York: Harper & Row, Pub., 1950), and John Dollard, et al., *Frustration and Aggression* (New Haven: Yale University Press, 1939).

5. See Richard Christie and Marie Jahoda (eds.), *Studies in the Scope and Methods of "The Authoritarian Personality"* (New York: Free Press, 1954), and Gordon W. Allport, *The Nature of Prejudice* (Reading, Mass.: Addison-Wesley, 1954).

6. The correlation coefficient, when squared, can be interpreted as the proportion of the variance in one variable associated with another. Thus a correlation of .3 means that only .09 of the variance in one variable is associated with a second variable, indicating that there is considerably more variance remaining to be explained. The concept of "variance" is also a technical term referring to a specific measure of dispersion about the arithmetic mean $\bar{x}$. The variance s^2 is defined as

$$s^2 = \frac{\sum\limits_{i=1}^{N} (x_i - \bar{x})^2}{N}$$

7. This was first pointed out by Edward A. Shils, "Authoritarianism: 'Right' and 'Left'," in Christie and Jahoda, *Studies in the Scope and Methods of "The Authoritarian Personality"*, pp. 24–49.

8. See Milton Rokeach, *The Open and Closed Mind* (New York: Basic Books, 1960).

9. Erich Fromm, *Escape from Freedom* (New York: Farrar, Straus & Giroux, 1942). See also, Erich Fromm, *Man for Himself* (New York: Holt, Rinehart and Winston, 1947).

10. Dollard, et al., *Frustration and Aggression*. For later formulations see Leonard Berkowitz, *Aggression: A Social Psychological Analysis* (New York: McGraw-Hill, 1962) and Albert Bandura, *Aggression: A Social Learning Analysis* (Englewood Cliffs, N.J.: Prentice-Hall, 1973).

11. See Robin M. Williams, Jr., *The Reduction of Intergroup Tensions* (New York: Social Science Research Council, 1947), p. 52.

12. See, for instance, Dee Brown, *Bury My Heart at Wounded Knee* (New York: Holt, Rinehart and Winston, 1970).

13. Some of this literature is summarized in Blalock and Wilken, *Intergroup Processes,* chap. 4.

14. For example, if there are three different goals involved, with utilities U_1, U_2 and U_3 respectively, and if the subjective probabilities of achieving these goals, given the behavior being evaluated, are p_1, p_2, and p_3 respectively, then the total subjective expected utility (SEU) for that behavior will be:

$$SEU = p_1 U_1 + p_2 U_2 + p_3 U_3$$

More accurately, these subjective probabilities will have to be compared with another set of probabilities associated with some alternative course of behavior, which in the simplest case may be that of nonaction. It is then postulated that the rational actor will behave so as to maximize the total SEU by selecting that behavioral alternative that yields the largest sum of these product terms.

15. Allport, *The Nature of Prejudice,* chap. 10.

16. Allport, *The Nature of Prejudice,* pp. 173-74.

17. Harold E. Quinley and Charles Y. Glock, *Anti-Semitism in America* (New York: Free Press, 1979), chaps. 3 and 10.

18. See Allport, *The Nature of Prejudice,* chap. 10.

19. A reference group is a group that serves as a focal point for the individual, regardless of whether or not he or she is an actual member. In the case of positive refer-

ence groups we presume that the individual would like to become a member and that the group's norms or behavior standards are positively endorsed by that actor.

20. For a discussion of the relationship between attitudes and behavior, as well as among the several attitudinal dimensions, see Howard J. Ehrlich, *The Social Psychology of Prejudice* (New York: Wiley, 1973).

21. Some of this literature is discussed in H. M. Blalock, *Toward a Theory of Minority-Group Relations* (New York: Wiley, 1967), chap. 2. See also Walter Kaufman, "Status, Authoritarianism, and Anti-Semitism," *American Journal of Sociology* 62 (1957), pp. 379–82.

CHAPTER 3
INEQUITABLE
EXCHANGES
INVOLVING
MINORITIES

The present chapter will be concerned with a number of differing exchange relationships between dominant and subordinate groups that are often referred to as "exploitative." Unfortunately, the notion of exploitation is difficult to define precisely, although generally it refers to the use of one party by another in such a fashion that the rate of exchange between them is considered "unfair"—that is, the exploiting party gains from the exchange a great deal more than the exploited party. Clearly, an "exchange" in which a slave works 12 to 15 hours a day in the cotton fields in return for a small amount of food and dilapidated housing would be considered unfair by nearly everyone. But what about a situation in which a person is paid low wages for unskilled labor and where, if that worker were to refuse to work, others would be happy to take his or her place? Is that "exploitation"? What about the student who claims "exploitation" by a faculty member because he or she is asked to do a certain amount of rather routine work? Much depends, in these latter instances, on just what rate of exchange is considered as fair, a matter that is likely to depend upon who is making the judgment.

What we are concerned with here is the problem of equity, about which a great deal has been written.[1] Ultimately, consideration of equity—or what constitutes a fair rate of exchange—come down to a subjective criterion based on judgments as to how much each person has invested in the exchange as compared with the returns received. This is why the subjective notion of "exploitation" is so difficult to define and why we prefer to use, instead, the term "inequitable exchange." The kinds of exchange with which we shall deal in this chapter are extreme, however, so much so that virtually all relatively neutral third parties would judge them as exploitative. They involve such forms of economic exchange as slavery, serfdom or debt bondage, the deliberate creation of surpluses of cheap labor, and the sexual abuse of minority-group women by dominant-group men. Even so, we shall use the term "exploitation" in quotes and only where it is evident from the context that we are referring to an unfair rate of exchange as *perceived* by one or more parties involved in that exchange.

In sociology equity theory stresses that actors in an exchange relationship expect to receive rewards or outcomes that are roughly proportional to their inputs or contributions; thus they will feel deprived, relative to others, whenever they believe they have made contributions disproportionate to their rewards. It is difficult, however, to compare the contributions that each party has made. Often these will be unknown, and usually they will be of a different nature. How does one compare the input of eight hours of work with a given amount of risk taken by a financial investor? And how can outcomes be compared, when one person's outcomes are in terms of income received, another's involve psychic satisfactions or reputation, and still another's amount to so much grain received for tenant farming on a given parcel of land? Clearly, there will be considerable room for disagreement concerning the fairness or equity of the exchange rate. Each party will have a vested interest in exaggerating the benefits awarded to the other, while underestimating its own investments.

It is a rare party indeed who will openly admit that an exchange has been "unfair" in the direction of favoring itself. Even in the case of slavery in the South, for example, the system was bolstered by an ideology that attempted to justify the arrangement in terms of its supposed benefits to the slaves. Slaves, it was argued, had been "saved" from a life of savagery and been bestowed with the benefits of Christianity. Similarly, the notion of the "White Man's Burden" became one of the ideological justifications for the colonial domination of Africa and Asia, whose indigenous populations were thus to be "civilized." On the other side, economically disadvantaged persons sometimes perceive as "exploitative" any kind of work arrangement under which they do not receive an income that to them seems "fair," regardless of the level of skill they bring to the job. Thus the notion of "exploitation" is in part a value judgment, as well as a political term used in ideological disputes. This does not mean, however, that all exchanges are judged equally fair by all observers. In fact, some—especially those imposed by force—will be considered extremely one-sided by virtually all third parties, regardless of how the immediate participants perceive them.

CAPITALISTIC VERSUS
NONCAPITALISTIC LABOR ARRANGEMENTS

Inequitable exchanges exist in many different forms and have been widely noted throughout human history. The types of exchange with which we shall be immediately concerned, however, are those that have emerged as a result of the spread of capitalistic economies, coupled with political controls stemming primarily from conquest. Prior to the rise of capitalism it happened many times that conquered peoples were physically removed from their homelands and placed into slavery. In other instances tribute has been extracted by conquering groups, the payments far in excess of the value of the "protection" the subordinate groups were afforded in exchange. In more recent times, especially in totalitarian states, unknown numbers of persons have been used to provide forced labor, often being fed only enough to barely survive at a minimum level and still be able to work. Many have died in these camps.

We know from historical evidence that large numbers of laborers were used periodically in most agrarian societies to work on massive public projects, such as irrigation canals and roads. Most likely they were used by rulers more interested in their own immortality or personal vanity than the welfare of their subjects. We know that vast hordes of laborers were pressed into service—unknown numbers dying in the process—to build and repair the Great Wall of China and also to construct a network of canals connecting the major Chinese rivers.[2] And although records are understandably incomplete, we can certainly imagine untold others being pressed into service as oarsmen for warships or as unskilled laborers used in constructing many of the world's finest churches, mosques, and temples. We also know that in most agrarian societies peasant classes have been forced to turn over as much as half of their crops to landlords or tax collectors. All of these forms of economic "exploitation" obviously predated modern capitalism. Furthermore they have not necessarily involved members of distinct racial or ethnic groups.

It is well to keep these facts in mind at the outset of the chapter, because there are a number of ideological theorists, particularly Marxists, who claim that economic "exploitation" is peculiar to capitalism and that, by implication, it would disappear under socialism. No one knows just how many persons worked and died in the forced labor camps under the regime of Joseph Stalin, nor are we ever likely to find out. Nor do we know how many were used, more recently, in a similarly brutal fashion by the Communist Pol Pot regime in Cambodia. We assume that economic policies are much less extreme today in the Communist countries of Eastern Europe, but here our conclusions would probably depend on what one considers a "fair" rate of exchange, as well as a more detailed knowledge of precisely how persons out of political favor in these countries have been treated. Nor do we know precisely what is currently going on in Vietnam or, for that matter, mainland China.

Marxist scholars are remarkably silent about such excessive practices, ones which have unaccountably occurred under a noncapitalistic system, perhaps because they, too, are ignorant of the true nature of those events. Nor do we have much good data concerning how many of the mistreated have been members of racial or ethnic minorities, rather than simply being those who are described as "political deviants." Soviet sociologists, for example, are deliberately vague and unspecific in discussing their own internal minorities, though we know that certain ethnic groups such as Ukrainians, Estonians, Latvians, and Georgians, as well as Soviet Jews, have periodically been suppressed. Clearly, a disproportionate number of the better-known Soviet dissidents are of the Jewish faith. Lacking any other evidence, we may assume that practices begun under the Czars which resulted in the notorious pogroms and the expulsion of millions of Jews have not yet disappeared and that extreme antisemitism within the USSR could flare up on relatively short notice.

Having said all these things, it is nevertheless clear that expanding capitalistic economic systems, coupled with nationalism, have produced a controversial record of very unequal exchange relationships throughout the world. Through historical accident, most of the relatively powerless peoples whose territories lay in the path of this capitalistic expansion were non-white, and thus many inequitable forms of capitalistic exchange have also been closely linked with racial domination. The history of black slavery in the United States, the Caribbean, and parts of Latin America are well known to American students. So is the story of the treatment of the American Indian. But other forms of capitalistic exchange, often considered as "exploitative," were also prevalent throughout most of what is today called the Third World. These included mining enterprises in Latin America and Africa, the extraction of tribute in Mexico and elsewhere, the development of cash-crop plantation economies in much of Africa and South Asia, and the use of exceedingly cheap "contract" labor in South Africa and in many of the less-developed countries. Today minority "exploitation" continues within the United States in the form of the poorly treated migrant labor force.

Modern capitalism has differed from other types of economies in terms of the extensiveness and persistence of its inequitable exchange systems. One of the distinctive differences has been the worldwide nature of the capitalistic market system, which has resulted in an economic division of labor in which whole countries and even subcontinents have become dependent on producing raw materials that have primarily benefited populations in the "developed" areas of the world.[3] Characteristically, the former economies are heavily dependent on a very small number of cash crops that are produced for a world market; prices for these goods may fluctuate considerably from one year to the next, with devastating implications for families that have, in the process, quit producing subsistence crops. In many of these countries, in fact, food must be imported to feed populations that exist at levels dangerously close to starvation. A drop in the price of their cash crops of even a few pennies may produce a major economic crisis.

The other side of this economic division of labor in the capitalistic world system has been the underdevelopment of local industries that might otherwise be capable of satisfying home markets for manufactured goods. The intrusion of the so-called "conglomerates" or multinational corporations into these countries has merely reinforced this pattern, with the major share of the profits being returned to stockholders residing in the industrial nations. Thus there has been a substantial net flow of raw materials out of the Third World regions, and, increasingly, leaders in these countries are complaining that they have not been receiving a fair share in return. Furthermore, many of these areas also suffer from depletion of mineral deposits and from soils that produce smaller and smaller amounts of agricultural products at increasingly greater costs.

These worldwide patterns do not, of course, necessarily involve minorities. Insofar as ethnic or racial minorities are in the most vulnerable positions, however, we may anticipate that they will be disproportionately affected. Many ethnic groups have been encouraged or even forced to migrate in order to supply the needed labor, thereby creating minority "problems" superimposed on more strictly economic ones. We shall discuss a few specific examples of this process shortly, but it should be emphasized that the pattern has been widespread. For instance, East Indians have been imported into the Caribbean, Japanese and Chinese to Hawaii and other western parts of the United States, and Mexicans have been encouraged to make illegal border crossings, all in order to maintain cheap supplies of labor during periods of relative labor scarcity. When this labor was no longer needed these migrants have then had to fend for themselves, often encountering the extreme hostility of other workers with whom they have found themselves in competition.

Although the best-known and most obvious examples of economic exchanges involving minorities took place during the European colonialist expansion into Africa and Asia in the nineteenth and early twentieth centuries, a number of internal U.S. minorities have been subjected to much the same kind of treatment. The term "internal colonialism" was popularized during the Civil Rights movement of the 1960s to draw attention to the "occupation" of black ghettos by white businesses, white-controlled police forces, and white city governments. Among sociologists the term also gained popularity with those who perceived far more similarities than differences in the treatment of colonial peoples and of minorities within our own country.[4]

Michael Hechter also used the term in the title of an important work that emphasizes how a division of labor may be imposed on peripheral regions of a country, so that core or dominant areas keep for themselves the major manufacturing, commercial, and banking roles and delegate to the peripheral regions the least profitable kinds of work, particularly the production of cash crops and the mining of coal or minerals useful in the manufacture of finished products.[5] If this regional division of labor is also closely linked to cultural differences, as is often the case, the two become confounded to produce a distinctive cultural division of labor. Those who perform the cheap labor come to be stereotyped as being naturally suited for that work; their religion or language is stigmatized; and in general they are assumed to possess an inferior culture which itself is partly blamed for the economic division of labor. Largely as a result, there is likely to be a counter-reaction by the minority ("reactive ethnicity") that persists over very long periods of time and that often crosscuts class differences within these regions.

Hechter's thesis is stated in general terms, but he applies it specifically to an "advanced" society, namely Great Britain. He provides considerable evidence to show that in many respects the so-called "Celtic fringe," consisting of Scotland, Wales, Ireland, and Northern Ireland, has served as a peripheral economic region, with industrial England the core. His thesis is that industrialization does not lead to eventual assimilation of ethnic groups and that cultural diffusion is often blocked by the reactive ethnicity in such peripheral regions. There may be outright political conflict, as occurred in the case of the Irish rebellion. But there may also be more subtle forms of resistance, as for example the refusal to give up native dialects or to join the established religion of the dominant core group.

The internal colonialism thesis calls to our attention the fact that exchange relationships perceived as "exploitative" may exist both between nation-states and within them. This thesis is not new and, indeed, has been emphasized by students of regional struggles within our own country. One sees obvious parallels, for example, between the Celtic fringe and the American South, as well as French-speaking areas of Canada. What deserves additional emphasis is the fact that such relationships may also occur *within* a single racial or ethnic group. Whenever these relationships are based on a territorial division of labor, however, there is likely to develop a set of beliefs and subcultural differences that serve as additional focal points of conflict. Some evidence of such subcultural differences is even apparent between the South and North, in spite of the fact that the white populations in these two regions originally stemmed from remarkably homogeneous origins. We can only speculate as to whether a really distinctive Southern "ethnic group" would have emerged had the economic division of labor between these regions continued for several more centuries.

SOME SPECIFIC TYPES OF ECONOMIC EXCHANGE

Slavery

Slavery is but one form of exchange based on political dominance, though undoubtedly the most extreme type. Slavery has usually been distinguished from other forms of bondage by virtue of the fact that slaves were owned outright as personal property and could be sold independently of the land on which they worked. In contrast, serfs ordinarily possessed certain rights relating to the land, as for example the right to till the land subject to the payment of a certain portion of the produce. Both slaves and serfs sometimes had additional legal rights, and there were also informal working arrangements that offered limited protections. Even under the harshest forms of slavery there were some regulations restricting the behavior of the owner. Of course, it was also to the economic advantage of the owner to protect his investment, at least to a limited degree. Some customs or laws even encouraged the manumission of slaves on the death of the master, or over a certain period of service, and in some instances—as for example in nineteenth-century Brazil—the number of manumissions was very substantial.[6] Nevertheless, slavery is distinguished from other kinds of labor arrangements because the slave was defined as personal property and practically always kept in this position by physical force.

It has been pointed out that slavery, as distinct from serfdom or contract labor, has usually been found in situations where cheap labor is highly profitable *and* simultaneously where such labor is relatively scarce. Nieboer has referred to such systems as involving "open resources."[7] This means that there is sufficient unused farming land so that individuals might fairly easily become independent farmers unless forced by some means to remain attached to a specific parcel of land. In such settings it often becomes necessary to import labor and to use force or legal means to retain control of this labor. Partly for historical reasons, and partly because racially different groups find it exceedingly difficult to escape or pass unnoticed into the local population, these imported slaves have usually been of a different race from that of the local population.

The most infamous enslavement of one people by another of course, was that of African slaves imported into the American South, the Caribbean, Brazil, and several other areas of Latin America. Prior to that efforts had been made in some parts of the Western Hemisphere to enslave the local Indians, but in those particular locations the indigenous peoples were too sparsely populated and too unaccustomed to agricultural labor to be suitable workers. Furthermore they could easily escape. In contrast, the Spanish invaders of Mexico found highly developed Indian civilizations with a sufficiently large population base to withstand the initial decimation produced by disease and warfare. These Indians turned out to be economically useful to their conquerors through a different type of exchange process that will be discussed below.[8]

It has been a characteristic of plantation economies and mining industries that the inefficiencies brought about by unskilled labor combined with the desire to produce quick profits have led to rather rapid depletion of resources. In the case of sugar, cotton, and the production of most other cash crops it therefore became the pattern to work the fields to their limit and then to move on to more productive soils. As long as land was plentiful, all was well and good. But, especially in the case of sugar production in the Caribbean islands—where space was obviously limited—this resulted in a sequence of rapid crop exploitation and then exhaustion. Initially a particular island would find itself in a very strong competitive position given its rich and productive soil. As this soil burned out, however, it would become increasingly necessary for plantation owners to push their slaves to the limit to compete with other islands where production had been started at a later date. At a still later point in time, the island would be totally priced out of the world market or placed at a severe competitive disadvantage, with the result the extreme poverty that even today characterizes much of the area. It indeed seems unbelievable to most Americans that this tiny area was once richer and far more important economically to England, France, and Spain than the rest of the New World combined.

These rather rapid changes in the productivity of this form of agriculture, when coupled with the territorial divisions among the several European powers, go a long way in explaining several important developments: the rise of the slave trade; England's considerable enthusiasm for this rather unusual type of commodity exchange; and that country's eventual opposition to this same trade once it became evident that it was beginning to work toward England's own disadvantage. Eric Williams, among others, has clearly documented the nature of the gains accruing to that country as a result of getting a head start in sugar production, primarily in Jamaica.[9]

Not only were there immense profits from sugar production itself, along with the rum consumption that it helped to encourage, but there were numerous side benefits as well. England's shipbuilding companies and seaports expanded considerably, as did the banking interests that invested in the slave trade. England's manufacturing also profited, though not nearly so much as later occurred in connection with the booming textile industries supplied by that other product of slave labor, King Cotton. It was not until England's arch rival France began to gain ground, as a result of Jamaica's depleted soil and the stronger competitive position of France's own sugar colonies, that the anti-slave-trade movement picked up momentum. Moralistic objections had been previously raised, of course. It was simply that they had never been compatible with the vested interests of those who were profiting handsomely from the slave trade.

The history of slavery in the American South and the rising importance of cotton to the British textile industries is much better known to American students. In this instance, as soils became depleted in Virginia, the Carolinas, and Georgia, it was possible to develop new plantations farther west, with the result that the heaviest concentrations of black slaves became located in the Mississippi delta region. Had the economic interests of the plantation owners not clashed with those of Northern industrialists, this westward expansion might have continued for several more decades. Sooner or later, however, cotton productivity in other parts of the world—also able to rely on exceedingly cheap labor—would undoubtedly have stopped the expansion.

One of the obvious disadvantages of slavery, as compared with other devices for utilizing cheap labor, is that it can be highly inefficient. As long as the soil is rich, the market strong, and competitors few, a system of slavery can be highly profitable. It can also be relatively efficient as long as the mere threat of force can be used to prevent uprisings, and as long as the supply of new slaves is plentiful. Given a sufficient supply, it may even be reasonably efficient to work one's slaves to exhaustion over a ten- to twenty-year period and to rely on a nearly all-male labor force. As this supply diminishes—as it did with the end of the slave trade—one must then rely on maintaining a high birth rate among slaves in order to replenish the supply. This is costly, however. Children must be clothed and fed, and their mothers will be removed from agricultural production for brief periods of time.

Today slavery has all but disappeared except, perhaps, in remote parts of the world where, even if still in existence, it cannot be extensive. It would be comforting to believe that the demise of slavery has been due to ethical objections and that "world opinion" would not stand for its reemergence. However, there are other forms of inequitable economic exchange that are almost as extreme and that are in many instances much more viable in regions of the world that have become heavily overpopulated. To these we now turn.

Serfdom and Debt Bondage

The differences between slavery, on the one hand, and certain other forms of economic exchange, on the other, can be very small. As noted, slavery is commonly distinguished by virtue of the fact that the slave is owned outright. There are several other devices by which economically dependent persons can be controlled and forced to engage in what are often considered "exploitative" exchanges. Most of these rely on combinations of economic and political controls that have the joint effect of keeping the dependent party locked into a life of toil and poverty. Where there is a substantial surplus of farm labor relative to available land, this may be accomplished by economic controls alone, since there will be a sufficient number of desperate families competing for work to ensure that very low rates of pay can be virtually guaranteed.

Under serfdom, families are in effect bound to parcels of land, which they work partly for themselves and partly for the owners or landlords. We commonly associate serfdom with medieval Europe and Asia, but a rather similar pattern existed within the Southern states in this country from the period immediately after the emancipation of the slaves in 1865 at least until World War II. Although no longer technically slaves, most blacks, as well as many poor whites in the South, found themselves in desperate economic situations following the Civil War. Unskilled, accustomed only to farm labor, and unable to purchase land of their own, these blacks and poor whites became "share croppers" tied to tiny parcels of land by a system of debt bondage that was strongly reinforced by local authorities and conveniently ignored by citizens in the rest of the country.[10]

Being illiterate and also unable to obtain loans at reasonable rates, these share croppers found themselves at the mercy of the owners of large parcels of land. They would have to purchase supplies in the local store, which charged high interest rates. Furthermore they were not in a position to challenge the "word" of their white landlord or store owner, who would often be the same person. Any black who did not accept the system ran the extreme risk of being imprisoned on trumped-up charges or of being beaten or even lynched. In good years the share cropper might break even or come out slightly ahead, but in poor seasons the debts would mount, so that it became next to impossible to break away from the system. Objectively speaking, many black and white Southern share croppers were no better off than true slaves. In theory they were free, but for all practical purposes they were trapped.

Where there is a large potential pool of unskilled labor that for some reason is not being tapped, another mechanism for forcing this labor supply into the market is to levy taxes that must be paid in cash, rather than in crops. This device has been effectively used in South Africa to induce tribal Africans to work as farm labor and in the mines.[11] Overpopulation in tribal reserves has had much the same result. Both taxation and overpopulation particularly force the younger males into the cities, mines, or white-owned farms as "temporary" labor. Many of these persons leave the tribal compound with the idea of earning just enough to pay the tax or to provide supplementary support for their kin. Some do move back and forth between the tribal and market economies, but many others become locked into the latter through the mechanism of incurring debts that are never totally repaid. Still others hire themselves out as contract labor, a subject that will be discussed below.

Tribute and Indirect Rule

Whenever an occupying or conquering party is able to take advantage of an already existing structure capable of supplying a surplus of products, some of which can be creamed off the top, a different means of economic exchange is feasible. It then becomes possible to work through the existing local hierarchy, making only minor adjustments to assure the loyalty of the appropriate persons, as for example village elders. Indirect rule is obviously less costly and much less disruptive of the existing productive system than slavery, serfdom, or a system of contract labor. It is especially tempting when the conquering group lacks the manpower to permit extensive settlement of the area or when the setting is highly unattractive to settlers from the conquering group. It depends, however, on the existing economy's ability to produce a surplus sufficient to justify the investment, as well as the cooperation of local leaders. The Spanish conquerors of Mexico relied on this technique. The British, in their control of India and colonies in West Africa and South Asia, were especially effective in their implementation of indirect rule which was basically a system of exchange that worked through the existing power structures in the colonized states. Where the climatic and geographic conditions encouraged the development of huge plantations producing cash crops for the world market, however, these patterns of indirect rule were supplemented by systems of contract labor or debt bondage.

Contract and Migrant Labor

Slavery, serfdom, and tribute systems have historically had some very serious drawbacks. Slaves must be clothed and fed, and their owners must be concerned with a host of details, including their physical health, the care for unproductive children and the aged, as well as mechanisms for preventing escape, and so forth. Serfs and share croppers, too, must be cared for in minimal ways. And because they are unlikely to be motivated to care properly for equipment and land, they may also engage in practices that deplete the soil too rapidly or that involve high repair costs. Especially in the case of highly seasonal work, where large numbers of hands are needed during very brief periods, these forms of labor can be expected to be competitive only when the soil is rich and there are few competitors relative to the demand. If this demand slackens, or if the agricultural crop or mineral being mined is being sold on the market much more cheaply by a competitor, some other productive system must be found.

Provided that a reliable but cheap source of labor can be made readily available at the appropriate times, it will obviously be much more efficient to hire persons by the hour or by a contract involving some piece-rate formula, for example, so much per amount picked or produced. That way, if too many persons show up for work, those who ask for too much or whose work is least efficient can be fired or turned away. When the work is completed, all can then be laid off and expected to fend for themselves. If child labor cannot be used, it is sometimes most efficient to encourage the migration of unmarried labor, persons who can live on a much lower income (and hence can be paid less) than those who would have to care for unproductive dependents. Thus in the nineteenth century when the railroads needed to be built during the rapid expansion of the American West, Chinese "coolie" labor was imported. Virtually all of these persons were young males. When their labor was no longer needed, they were left to drift for themselves, and, of course, many found their way to the urban areas of the west coast, where they were accused of undercutting white labor.[12]

With contract or migrant labor the employer's basic problem is to assure that a sufficiently large labor supply is available so that the wages demanded can yield a reasonable profit. In an expanding economy, such as existed in the United States during the eighteenth and nineteenth centuries, this is not always easy. Just as one source of cheap labor seems assured, expanding opportunities permit alternatives to those workers so that another group must be found. It is thus very common to find that such labor is contracted *outside* of the area often of the same ethnic group, by labor recruiters, who deliberately mislead potential migrants about not only the contract itself but also about the conditions under which they will be working. Furthermore, the aim is to recruit far more persons than are actually needed, so as to have available a convenient reserve. Once recruited, these migrants will then find themselves in situations of intense competition, both with each other and with other earlier immigrants whom they may be undercutting. If there is a subsequent recession, throwing persons who are native to the area out of work, the hostilities between these natives and the newcomers may become intense.

These outsiders need not, of course, be members of distinct racial groups. John Steinbeck's classic novel, *The Grapes of Wrath* (1940), depicts the plight of the "Okie" farmers migrating to southern California during the Great Depression.[13] The Joad family, and others whom they encountered along the migratory route, found themselves deluged with handbills promising plenty of good work in California. When they arrived, however, they found that they had been deliberately misled, drawn by false promises into further flooding the pool of cheap Western labor, thus taking part in what amounted to a continuous process of underbidding their fellow migrants in a desperate effort to obtain a few days' work. Carey McWilliams, in *Ill Fares the Land* (1941), documents how the same pattern portrayed vividly by Steinbeck was occurring in many other places throughout the country.[14]

Migrant labor today still constitutes a very serious social problem within the United States. These migrants include many poor whites as well as blacks and Hispanics. Migrant streams still exist along the east coast and within the Midwest, but perhaps the most severe instance of competition between a native labor force and migrants occurs in California and, to a lesser degree, in the Pacific Northwest. Intimately linked with the problem of the illegal entry of millions of Mexican "wetbacks," migrant competition creates a serious policy dilemma for the American government.

When the problem of Mexican immigration is examined closely, it is economic and demographic factors that we see at the base of this delicate political problem. Migrant labor is still "needed" at harvest times in very large quantities for brief periods of time. Illegal Mexican immigrants make especially desirable candidates for cheap labor, since for many of them the wages paid are higher than those to which they are accustomed and since they dare not protest low wages for fear of risking being returned. These facts are clearly recognized both by illegal migrant employers and by those who are attempting to organize the agricultural labor force in California. Unfortunately, this situation often pits Chicano against Chicano. Those who are American born, or who have either achieved citizenship or have entered legally, are undercut by illegal workers who have just arrived and who are accustomed to a much lower standard of living.

The very high birth rate in Mexico, coupled with its unemployment and underemployment, have produced a large population of potential migrants, many of whom are virtual squatters in Tiajuana and other border cities. Given the extensive border between the two countries plus the sensitive diplomatic issues involved, it becomes virtually impossible to control this immigration effectively. When we add to this the fact that many employers in California and other Southwestern states have vested economic interests in encouraging the entry of this cheap supply of labor—at least at certain times of the year—we can easily understand why little or nothing is being done to reduce this flow of immigrants.[15] The migratory "push" from the Mexican side will remain strong until that country begins to lower its birth rate and develops its economy. The "pull" from the North seems to be gradually reducing, however, as the need for large supplies of cheap labor subsides due to increasing mechanization and automation of agricultural production and distribution.[16]

Cheap Industrial Labor

The industrial revolution began in the eighteenth and nineteenth centuries, bringing swift and wideranging change to many nations. Initially the rise of large industries required very large numbers of unskilled laborers and miners, many of whom worked long hours under arduous and dangerous conditions. These early industrial workers in England and France were not ethnically or even religiously distinct from the much smaller class of persons who benefited from their labors; they were instead simply those who were least able to compete effectively for the relatively small number of better positions. A large proportion had been displaced from overpopulated rural areas. Many were women and young children, whose life expectancies and health suffered tremendously as a result. Thus it should not be assumed that the issues with which we are concerned are peculiar to minorities.

Today, in many parts of the world, there are swelling urban populations that have also been produced by rural overpopulation. Changes brought on by the industrial revolution—linked to improved health facilities and medical knowledge, transportation networks that have prevented starvation in local areas, and the virtual elimination of mass epidemics—have resulted in a very much lowered death rate. Coupled with moderately high birth rates, this has permitted a prodigious increase in the world's population. Much of this population hovers on the brink of starvation, and most certainly there is considerable underemployment in virtually all nonindustrialized rural economies.

This surplus underemployed population has moved to the cities in search of jobs. The net result has been a huge surplus of urban unskilled labor that can readily be tapped at extremely low wages. Moreover, this urbanward migration has resulted in the contacts of many different ethnic groups, all vying for a relatively small number of positions. Thus although racial and ethnic relations are, in one sense, only a "side issue" in this competitive process, the arena is one in which tensions among such groups can be expected to occur. Furthermore, employers can and often do play one group off against another, in an effort to keep wages as low as possible and to inhibit cooperation among them. In short, the situation in many parts of the world is ripe for interethnic hostilities derived from this competition.

Between roughly the middle of the nineteenth century and World War II the United States witnessed a minor illustration of this process which, fortunately for those involved, was coupled with both geographic and economic expansion that considerably reduced the strains involved. In effect, America became the safety-valve for Europe by syphoning off Europe's excess populations. The Irish immigrants were the prototype of several other groups that arrived on our shores slightly later. These were former peasants who had suffered untold economic hardships, as well as domination by the English; the situation had reached a climax around 1846 when potato famines forced several waves of them to leave their small plots of land for a totally strange urban environment along the Eastern seaboard of America.

Oscar Handlin, among others, has portrayed their story in vivid fashion.[17] His history suggests striking parallels between the hardships the Irish immigrants faced and those encountered by our present nonwhite minorities. They worked extremely long hours, women and young children as well as men, under harsh and even dangerous conditions. Their jobs could be taken away at any time, and their living conditions were unhealthy. Winning even their own children's respect was hard, not only because the parents lacked command of the native language and belonged to a minority religious group, but also because of the many negative stereotypes that these children had to cope with in their daily lives. Other white ethnic immigrant groups soon followed and experienced many of the same difficulties, though apparently to somewhat lesser degrees with each new wave of arrivals.

These immigrant groups supplied a steady source of cheap industrial labor. Although each successive wave suffered hardships, no single ethnic group experienced extreme hardship, collectively, for more than a generation or two. Characteristically, the second generations for the most part became semiskilled and skilled laborers. Many of these white ethnic groups, taking advantage of cultural patterns that provided them with particular skills, began to specialize and move into occupational niches that gave each group additional means of leverage. The Irish, for example, moved into politics to such an extent that they are even today stereotyped as being "glad-handers" and just a bit corrupt. Many Italians became successful truck farmers and grocers.

After immigration from Eastern and Southern Europe was virtually cut off in the 1920's—remaining relatively light to the present day—their place was taken by blacks, Puerto Ricans, and Chicanos, all of whom are physically more identifiable than the white ethnic immigrants. As the American economy showed signs of slowing down, it became apparent that there might not be any new waves of immigrants, so that the newest groups tended to be locked at the bottom. Although perhaps a few of their members would move up the ladder slightly, being replaced by other members of the *same* ethnic groups, black, Puerto Rican, and Chicano groups would continue to be stigmatized, since prejudiced persons would be unlikely to distinguish the few middle-class members of these minorities from the others. Residential segregation would merely reinforce this apparent lack of differentiation within each group. For example, all blacks would seem alike. Thus it appeared that the new nonwhite immigrants were to supply a more or less permanent unskilled labor pool to feed what seemed to be an equally permanent need for cheap U.S. labor.

It is now becoming apparent that things are not working out this way, though the net result may be nearly the same. In the United States and most of the other industrialized nations the need for cheap labor, even in rural areas, has been declining at a very rapid rate. What is occurring is that unskilled persons are becoming redundant and therefore useless to the labor force. As minimum wages rise, for example, a certain number of persons are priced out of the private-sector labor force for the simple reason that it does not pay to hire them. Much of this reduction in the need for unskilled labor is due to automation as well as to the greater demands for technically skilled employees and white-collar workers in the growing service sector of our economy. Likewise, women who previously contributed their work entirely through the household economy are entering the labor force and taking up these technical positions. Those who lack the necessary skills—or who are blocked from getting them through discrimination—are increasingly unable to find any work in the private sector at all.

Blacks, Hispanics, American Indians, some but not all Asian-Americans, and certain pockets of underprivileged whites are disproportionately represented among these unemployed. For example, the black unemployment rate has consistently been double that of whites for the past three decades.[18] "Unemployment," as defined by the U.S. Census, is a misleading term, however, since only those who claim to be actively seeking work are eligible to be counted as unemployed. Those who have given up hope, or who pop into the labor force only very sporadically when a temporary job becomes available, are only rarely counted. Thus the true unemployment rates for all categories are higher than those reported. We therefore do not know what the true ratio of black to white unemployed really is, but it seems reasonable to assume that it is even greater than two to one. Estimates of the true unemployment rates for black teenagers and young adults range as high as 30 to 50 percent!

Thus in the United States the problem of labor "exploitation" may be solving itself, thanks to industrialization and automation, but at the expense of unemployment for the unskilled. As Sidney Willhelm has pointed out in his book, *Who Needs the Negro?*, a high percentage of blacks may soon become redundant in terms of the private-sector economy.[19] If so, the implications are indeed bleak *unless* ways can be found to absorb these and other persons into public-sector jobs. But these would have to be something other than "meaningless" jobs that are obvious dead ends.[20] But will economy-minded voters and elected officials be willing to underwrite such a program? It would indeed be tragic if we are finally in a position to end what many consider economic "exploitation" within our own country, only to replace it with a form of neglect that has equally dire consequences for millions of Americans, whites as well as racial minorities.

SEXUAL CONTACTS BETWEEN
DOMINANT AND SUBORDINATE GROUPS

Sexual relations between dominant-group males and subordinate-group females have occurred quite frequently throughout history. From the standpoint of racial and ethnic relations we may restrict our focus to two implications that this particular kind of relationship will almost inevitably have. First, it results in a certain number of mixed-blood offspring who, as we noted earlier, must be "placed" in some fashion within the social structure. In Brazil, where initially there were very few white women and where interracial unions were extensive, this resulted in a relatively large group of mulatto offspring who became an intermediate group in the social structure.[21] Over several generations, with intermarriages among various color combinations, this resulted in a social structure in which color became defined along a *continuum*. This is in sharp contrast with the situation in the United States, where these children were defined as racially "black," regardless of the actual shade of their skin color. As we noted earlier, these mixed-bloods were needed to fill intermediate positions in the Brazilian economy, which they could do without encountering the opposition of an already existent group of poor whites.[22]

The second consequence of this form of sexual contact is more psychological, but with important implications for the family structure of the subordinate group. Sexual relations of this type are not only humiliating to the female partner but also to the subordinate-group male who is unable to protect her.[23] Jealousies and accusations, as well as genuine doubts as to biological inheritances, inevitably arise. Minority males naturally distrust those women from their own group who have "given" sexual favors to the hated dominant males, and at the same time they are concerned about their own sexual adequacy. Minority women in effect have a weapon to use if they so desire, and, because of the status differences involved, "whiteness" easily becomes a desired attribute. Even children born of the same parents but having different skin colors often find themselves ranked according to this attribute. It is only very recently that the notion that "black is beautiful" has taken hold among American blacks. Even so, one still notices advertisements in black-oriented magazines that attempt to sell "whiteness" and that imply that "white" hairstyles are to be emulated. Thus a by-product of these sexual relationships, whether perceived as "exploitative" or not, has been a whole set of psychological concerns relating to one's ancestry and to skin color in particular. The ego of the minority male inevitably suffers, and when one adds to this the fact that discrimination in other respects also makes it difficult for these men to support their families adequately, it should come as no surprise that severe strains may develop.

On the other side, sexual relationships between dominant-group males and subordinate-group females can also be expected to be resented by dominant-group females. Characteristically, we find in such settings that dominant-group females are placed on a pedestal, so to speak, and seen as pure and overly virtuous. Thus, especially in the South, a sharp line used to be drawn between the promiscuous black female and her purified, and probably extremely jealous, white counterpart. Neither category of women gained from the imagery, of course, but the latter at least extracted certain privileges from the patterns of chivalry that often accompanied it.

Finally, there is often an exaggerated fear that subordinate-group males will gain the ultimate revenge through rape as a form of aggression. This fear of rape of white women by black men became one of the "ultimate" justifications for the severe system of social controls that existed throughout the South following emancipation and that reached its height in the several decades following 1890. Fear of rape became the most common reason for the lynchings that reached an annual level as high as 150 during the 1890s.[24] Though the lynchings have disappeared, the fear still remains to an unknown degree, though it is not explicitly mentioned in polite white society. It is basically a fear of black aggression.

Extensive asymmetric sexual contacts across groups are only possible when there are extreme inequalities of power between dominant and subordinate groups. They are also much less likely in situations where the sex ratio within the dominant group is reasonably balanced. Therefore, they have been primarily characteristic of settings in which there have been only a very few whites (or other dominant groups) occupying superordinate positions in advance of the immigration of larger numbers of permanent settlers. Such was the case in the Brazilian plantation economy, and it has also occurred in those parts of South Asia where relatively small numbers of white plantation managers, soldiers, and civil servants were needed to extract profits and keep order, but where white women failed to settle in proportionate numbers.

In South Asia there resulted a number of so-called "Eurasian" offspring who tended to be absorbed into the economy in intermediate social positions. Many of these Eurasian descendents of mixed unions found themselves torn between two cultural traditions, trying to make it into the dominant white elite but never quite being accepted. In several parts of the world, these mixed-bloods then found themselves in a very difficult position when the European colonial powers withdrew from these areas in the period immediately following World War II.[25]

In the United States we may assume that, except in rare cases, these types of forced sexual contacts have all but vanished. But it may be several more decades before the resulting resentment also subsides and perhaps even longer before the indirect effects on minority families and individual self-respect have also disappeared. One of the important consequences of the Black Power movement of the 1960s, with its attendant emphasis on racial pride, may have been to accelerate this process in the case of this particular minority.

INEQUITABLE EXCHANGES AND CHOICE BEHAVIOR

Having discussed a number of types of inequitable exchanges, we must now draw the argument together in terms of choice behavior, utilities, subjective probabilities and the interdependencies that exist between dominant and subordinate groups. Extreme exchanges of the types we have considered obviously require a considerable power differential between the parties involved, a fact which often makes racial and ethnic minorities highly vulnerable candidates for such "exploitation." Other less extreme, and far more common, arrangements usually involve much smaller power differentials in which the party that receives the lesser benefits from the exchange is nevertheless still able to extract a sufficient number of concessions to make the exchange reasonably worthwhile.

We have already noted that both slave and cheap contract labor are usually highly inefficient and costly in a number of ways, especially in terms of care for equipment and in assuring that soil will remain productive over a number of years. Plantation economies have characteristically involved shortsighted farming techniques that have tended to exhaust the land. As long as alternative land has been available this has done no special harm. But sooner or later, in almost every area that this mode of production has been extensively used, a point has been reached where the soil was no longer sufficiently productive to ensure a profit in the face of competitors from other regions. In some instances, as in the rubber plantations of Malaysia, a substitute product (in this case synthetic rubber) has created such a drop in the market price that the plantation economy has suffered severe setbacks.

Thus, although the dominant party may have virtual control over the subordinate one, *both* parties can find themselves in a situation in which they are mutually dependent on a larger system. That is, they both lack alternative means. A drop in the market price or in productivity may mean financial ruin for the owner unless this productivity can somehow be increased dramatically. One alternative—and the one that will be most likely sought as an immediate solution—is that of extracting even more work out of one's slaves or labor force. But there are clearly limits beyond which this solution will have only marginal value. A second alternative is to cut corners, either by lowering wages or reducing the value of goods supplied to one's labor force: for example, reductions in food rations, in housing quality, in medical services, and so forth. Both of these solutions, of course, make the system even more harsh and increase the likelihood of either an overt rebellion or more subtle forms of sabotage. It is the *inability* of the dominant party, due to a lack of economic power, to cope directly with this market situation that, in effect, requires the additional application of force or power over the subordinate party. It is in this sense that the dominant party is also dependent on the relationship. The mutual interdependence between the two parties is thus a result of the economic system.

A third alternative, which will ultimately imply the termination or extensive modification of the exchange arrangement, is to reduce one's dependence on the particular crop or mineral in question or to find substitutes. The boll weevil —a pest that nearly threatened to destroy the Southern cotton crop during the 1920s—has been credited as being one major impetus behind the South's move to diversify its agricultural products and, over a period of several decades, greatly to increase its average standard of living as a result.[26] As other parts of the world have come to replace the South in cotton production, this need for very cheap Southern labor, both white and black, has gradually been modified.

Still another alternative—which was not open to American plantation owners during the period of slavery or its aftermath—is that of mechanizing and automating so that a very few machines can replace the labor of hundreds of unskilled workers. This alternative has since become possible for an increasing number of agricultural crops, as well as mining industries, thereby freeing the employer from dependence upon unskilled labor. But this, of course, also forces those who have been displaced to find alternative means of support, if they can do so. If they cannot, their own dependence may simply be transferred to another source, whether this be another type of employer who needs their cheap labor or a government that must find alternative means of support.

In the case of an employer—for example, a plantation owner or a corporation relying on cheap migrant labor and producing a cash crop for the market—the *utilities* for continuing the labor exchange relationship will be a function of the market price, which in turn will be a function of supply and demand. If these crops can be produced at a substantial profit there will be a considerable motivation to do so, regardless of the means required. If it is also true that there are very few alternative means, so that the subjective probabilities of achieving these goals by this particular means are considerably higher than any others, then we have the "perfect" conditions for a system that many consider "exploitative." As long as these agricultural producers can exert sufficient power on their own governments, and as long as these governments themselves remain powerful vis-a-vis other governments, the system will almost certainly remain in place. There may be idealistic arguments raised against the exploitative arrangement, whether it be slavery or the use of cheap migrant labor, but there will generally be too many who indirectly benefit from it—bankers, merchants, huge corporations, and ordinary citizens who enjoy the cheap prices.

Minorities or other subordinate groups also have very little choice in these situations. Overt rebellions, though always a threat, are easily suppressed given the very great power inequalities. Therefore the most common mode of adjustment is that of passive resignation, combined with whatever subtle types of noncooperation can be managed—work slowdowns, deliberate incompetence, or unexplainable sabotage. In this type of situation the individual minority member must seek protection from whatever benefactor he or she can find, and this practically always results in a paternalistic relationship in which the subordinate party must play the role of a highly subservient and overtly loyal dependent—in a fashion reminiscent of feudalistic relationships between lord and vassal. Pierre van den Berghe, in his *Race and Racism*, has, in fact, referred to race relations situations of this type as "paternalistic," in contrast with what he calls "competitive" ones that are much more characteristic of industrial societies.[27]

In effect, in these situations there is no real choice at all. All parties are locked into the arrangement until outside market factors and soil depletion begin to make the arrangement less profitable. At that point, alternatives may be sought. If mechanization and automation procedures are instituted soon enough, the particular crop may continue to be produced by a very different kind of arrangement. Otherwise, when the crop (or mining operation) ceases to make a reasonable profit the system will be undermined. Straightforward economic arguments seem entirely sufficient to explain the phenomena under discussion in this chapter.

As we have already suggested, currently in the United States the use of cheap labor is relatively infrequent and has been undergoing a rather steady decline. But elsewhere in the world many plantation crops are still being produced by economies still playing a peripheral economic role to the so-called "core" countries, supplying them with the raw materials for their industries, as well as specialized food products for the world economy. This situation may also change, though there are some who argue that this is not likely to happen as long as the world economy remains capitalistic in nature.[28]

There are, however, a number of American industries and farming enterprises that still depend on cheap labor. We have already noted the case of migrant agricultural labor needed to harvest perishable crops during very brief seasons of the year. Other industries, such as the "fast food" chains, rely heavily on the labor of students and other young people. Many would not ordinarily refer to such situations as being "exploitative," however. There are also still some traditional unskilled service roles that cannot be automated easily: maids in hotels and motels, clean-up employees in hospitals, custodians, and so forth. Certain industries, such as the textile mills in the South, still employ large numbers of nonunionized and unskilled or semiskilled workers at very low wages. Other businesses must employ additional workers at peak seasons, for example, during the Christmas holidays. And of course there are many "female" occupations—such as those of secretary, file clerk, elementary school teacher, librarian, or nurses' aid—that receive much lower wages than male-dominated occupations involving comparable skill levels.

Some economists have used the term "dual labor market" to refer to the distinction between "primary" industries and "secondary" ones.[29] Primary industries are capital intensive (that is, they rely heavily on machines and automation), derive greater profits than other industries, and are able to employ a well-paid and highly skilled labor force. Secondary industries, in contrast, still rely on cheap labor, are labor intensive, and tend to reap lower profits. Because of the relationship between profit and the use of a capital-intensive strategy, we would naturally expect secondary-industry employers to strive toward automation. But not all industries are capable of doing so, for technical reasons as well as less practical ones. Service work in particular may not lend itself to such automation. Thus, such services will either become highly expensive (as is the case with medical and educational services) or they will rely on a labor force that is underpaid to keep costs to their customers down.

Whether or not one wishes to refer to service workers as "exploited" will, as we have implied, be a subjective judgment—that is, whether they are receiving a fair return for their work. It does seem highly likely, however, that racial and ethnic minorities will continue to constitute a disproportionate number of these persons in secondary industries. White women have also, in the past, been overrepresented in this category, but we may predict that their leverage for climbing out of these positions will be far greater than that of blacks, Hispanics, American Indians, and several of the Asian-American groups.

NOTES

1. Some of this literature is summarized in Blalock and Wilken, *Intergroup Processes,* chap. 6. See especially: Peter M. Blau, *Exchange and Power in Social Life* (New York: Wiley, 1964); George C. Homans, *Social Behavior: Its Elementary Forms,* rev. ed. (New York: Harcourt Brace Jovanovich, Inc., 1974); and Karen S. Cook and Toby L. Parcel, "Equity Theory: Directions for Future Research," *Sociological Inquiry,* 47 (1977), pp. 75–88.

2. See L. Carrington Goodrich, *A Short History of the Chinese People,* 4th ed. (New York: Harper & Row, Pub., 1969).

3. See Daniel Chirot, *Social Change in the Twentieth Century* (New York: Harcourt Brace Jovanovich, Inc., 1977); and Immanuel Wallerstein, *The Modern World-System: Capitalist Agriculture and the Origins of the European World-Economy in the Sixteenth Century* (New York: Academic Press, 1976).

4. For an expository discussion of the notion of internal colonialism see Robert Blauner, "Internal Colonization and Ghetto Revolt." *Social Problems,* 16 (1969), pp. 393–408.

5. Michael Hechter, *Internal Colonialism: The Celtic Fringe in British National Development, 1536–1966* (Berkeley: University of California Press, 1975).

6. See: Donald Pierson, *Negroes in Brazil;* and Philip Mason, *Patterns of Dominance* (London: Oxford University Press, 1970), chap. 13.

7. H. J. Nieboer, *Slavery as an Industrial System* (The Hague: Martinus Nijhoff, 1910 ed.).

8. For an excellent comparative analysis of inequitable exchange systems in Central and Latin America see Charles Wagley and Marvin Harris, *Minorities in the New World* (New York: Columbia University Press, 1958); see also Mason, *Patterns of Dominance,* chaps. 11–13.

9. Eric Williams, *Capitalism and Slavery.*

10. See E. Franklin Frazier, *The Negro in the United States* (New York: Macmillan, 1957), chaps. 7 and 10; and Gunnar Myrdal, *An American Dilemma* (New York: Harper & Brothers, 1944) chaps. 10 and 11.

11. See Philip Mason, *Patterns of Dominance*, chap. 9; and Pierre L. van den Berghe, *Race and Racism: A Comparative Perspective* (New York: Wiley, 1967), chap. 5.

12. See James W. Vander Zanden, *American Minority Relations* (New York: Ronald Press, 1963), chaps. 5 and 9; Lewis H. Carlson and George A. Colburn (eds.), *In Their Place: White America Defines Her Minorities, 1850-1950* (New York: Wiley, 1972), part 4; and Stanford Lyman, *Chinese Americans* (New York: Random House, 1974), chap. 4.

13. John Steinbeck, *The Grapes of Wrath* (New York: Viking Press, 1939).

14. Carey McWilliams, *Ill Fares the Land* (New York: Barnes and Noble, 1941).

15. See Michael Burawoy, "The Functions and Reproduction of Migrant Labor: Comparative Material from Southern Africa and the United States," *American Journal of Sociology,* 81 (1976), pp. 1050-87.

16. For a case study involving the lettuce industry see William H. Friedland, Amy E. Barton, and Robert J. Thomas, *Manufacturing Green Gold: The Conditions and Social Consequences of Lettuce Harvest Mechanization* (Cambridge University Press, in press).

17. Oscar Handlin, *The Uprooted* (New York: Grosset and Dunlap, 1951); and *Boston's Immigrants* (Cambridge, Mass: Belknap Press, 1959).

18. See Reynolds Farley, "Trends in Racial Inequalities: Have the Gains of the 1960's Disappeared in the 1970's," *American Sociological Review,* 42 (1977), pp. 189–208.

19. Sidney M. Willhelm, *Who Needs the Negro?* (Garden City, N. Y.: Anchor Books, 1971).

20. For a more detailed statement see H. M. Blalock, *Black-White Relations in the 1980's,* chap. 7.

21. See Donald Pierson, *Negroes in Brazil,* chaps. 4-6; and Philip Mason, *Patterns of Dominance,* chap. 13.

22.   In Hawaii, also, there was extensive intermarriage among several groups, including Native Hawaiians, Chinese, Japanese, Filipinos, and whites, thus making it almost impossible to draw distinct lines among groups. See Romanzo Adams, *Intermarriage in Hawaii* (New York: Macmillan, 1937) and Bernhard Hormann, "Hawaii's Mixing People," in Gist and Dworkin (eds.) *The Blending of Races* (New York: Wiley, 1972).

23.   See John Dollard, *Caste and Class in a Southern Town* (New York: Doubleday, 1949). Frazier, in particular, has emphasized the effects this sexual relationship has had on black families. See E. Franklin Frazier, *The Negro Family in the United States* (University of Chicago Press, 1939). For a more recent discussion see Andrew Billingsley, *Black Families in White America* (Englewood Cliffs, N. J.: Prentice-Hall, 1968).

24.   E. Franklin Frazier, *The Negro in the United States,* pp. 159–64.

25.   See Noel P. Gist and Anthony G. Dworkin (eds.), *The Blending of Races.* The "classic" work on such marginal peoples was Everett V. Stonequist's *The Marginal Man: A Study in Personality and Culture Conflict* (New York: Scribner's, 1937).

26.   See Gunnar Myrdal, *An American Dilemma,* pp. 234–35.

27.   Pierre L. van den Berghe, *Race and Racism,* pp. 25–34.

28.   See especially Immanuel Wallerstein, *The Modern World-System.*

29.   See Robert T. Averitt, *The Dual Economy: The Dynamics of American Industry Structure* (New York: Horton, 1968); and Richard C. Edwards, Michael Reich, and David M. Gordon, *Labor Market Segmentation* (Lexington, Mass.: Heath, 1975).

CHAPTER 4
COMPETITION
AND DISCRIMINATION

Although strictly economic theories may account for exchange relationships very adequately where the parties have few real choices, it is much more difficult to deal with the phenomenon of competition. From the standpoint of the individual, there are many actual and potential competitors, only a few of whom are members of racial or ethnic minorities. How does this competition come to be defined along *group* lines in these instances? Under what conditions will individuals attempt to place roadblocks in the paths of certain other competitors, rather than competing strictly as individuals? And under what conditions will coalitions among persons in similar competitive positions be formed? These are some of the questions that need to be addressed in this chapter.

Suppose a qualified individual trains for admission into a graduate or professional school, and suppose that he or she is turned down—probably with a polite letter stating that since many other excellent candidates have also applied only a small proportion could be selected. Although we would naturally expect this individual to be disappointed, we would also assume that the selection process has been fair and that those selected were simply better qualified. The reasonable applicant would then quietly go back home and reapply for some other position or program, eventually succeeding in locating an appropriate job or an opening in a lesser program. The competition would be defined in individual terms.

Competition, however, can also take place between groups. A hypothetical white male's chances of being accepted for that same graduate school obviously would be at least somewhat improved if certain classes of competitors, say blacks and white women, could be ruled out, or at least handicapped to a considerable degree. Usually the applicants themselves have no power to impose such restrictions. But if certain of their competitors stand out in some manner, and if those who are making the selections are also members of the same group or category as the first group of applicants, such informal discriminatory practices might be expected. But this will depend upon the interests of the selectors and how these may diverge from those of the applicants. The situation becomes highly complex and subject to a number of noneconomic influences.

In this chapter we shall discuss a number of factors that affect whether or not competition is defined along group lines and, if so, what the implications are for minorities. These factors include: (1) whether groups are dichotomized and a split labor market created; (2) the nature of the initial contacts and division of labor with the minority; (3) resentment of the minority's success; (4) the minority's size and geographic concentration; and (5) certain characteristics of the occupation or setting. The chapter concludes with a brief discussion of certain trends in impersonal factors that have affected minorities' relative competitive resources.

DICHOTOMIES AND THE SPLIT LABOR MARKET

One important indicator of group competition is the degree to which the competitors come to be dichotomized along certain highly visible lines. If competitors are strung out along a continuum, as for example by ability or age, it is difficult to make and justify sharp distinctions among them. Contrast this with, say, religious distinctions between Protestants and Catholics, Jews and Muslims, or Hindus and Muslims. As we have noted previously, in Brazil there is no clear dichotomy between "blacks" and "whites," but instead there is a finely graded set of terms capable of distinguishing among various shadings of skin color; this continuum does not lend itself to sharp distinctions of group or class. In contrast, where a dichotomy does exist it is much easier to establish simple rules by which one category gets certain privileges denied to the other. Sometimes these rules may be open and explicit, though usually they are simply "understood." In our own country, at least until very recently, it was "understood" that a woman employee would receive a lower salary than a male counterpart in the same job and that she would probably not be promoted above a certain level.

In the job sphere this dichotomization makes possible what has been termed a "split labor market"; competition is regulated by the simple device of allocating certain jobs to one category and a different set to the other.[1] If the actual work that each category does is basically similar, the same result can be accomplished by a distinction in job titles, together with a well-defined status distinction between them. For instance, where blacks and whites have been hired together in construction crews within the South, it was once customary—in fact, mandatory—to designate the black workers as helpers or assistants.

Along with this simplified division of labor usually goes a substantial pay differential that creates certain strains among three parties: high-paid workers, low-paid workers, and employers. In South Africa, for instance, the ratio of black, or "Native," pay levels to those of whites has been on the order of one to ten or one to fifteen.[2] Today in the United States evidence indicates that persons in so-called "female fields"—and this includes a few men, of course—earn around 75 percent as much as persons in male-dominated fields of approximately the same skill or experience level. Such a split market makes it very tempting for employers to hire members of the low-paid category at the expense of those from the favored group, thus pitting one category of employees against the other.

One defense used by high-paid workers against this device is political: getting the government to pass regulations that place strict limits on how many or what kinds of persons can be hired in each category. This has in fact occurred in South Africa. A second device is to attempt to get the lower-paid category excluded altogether from employment. This may be accomplished through legislation, threats and acts of violence, or legal restrictions on immigrant groups' entry to the country. The movements to prevent Chinese and later Japanese immigration to the United States (after the period when they were no longer "needed" for cheap labor) is an example of this latter strategy. It was *labor* groups—meaning *white* labor, of course—that were largely behind this west coast effort to regulate "unfair" Asian immigrant competition.[3]

Still another though less common device has been noted by Bonacich in the case of these split-market situations. This is the establishment of a caste or castelike system along the lines of that which has existed in India. In the extreme this would involve a rigidly defined division of labor among a hierarchy of castes, with the system being reinforced by various forms of control that serve to perpetuate the hierarchical system and inhibit occupational competition. If there are only two or three distinct categories of persons, it is feasible to create a hierarchical castelike system with a rigid division of labor and pay differentials. The situation that existed between blacks and whites in the South prior to World War II has been described as having many such castelike features, though the extent of the similarities and differences between this sort of system and the much more complex one in India has been a subject of considerable debate that need not concern us here.[4]

INITIAL GROUP CONTACTS:
AFFECT ON DIVISION OF LABOR

Another factor influencing the extent to which competition is likely to be defined along group rather than individualistic lines is that of the historical conditions under which the groups first came into contact and the nature of the initial division of labor. Racial and ethnic groups often meet under dramatic circumstances resulting from mass migrations or conquest.[5] If so, their distinctive differences will be obvious to all. It is also likely that one group will be in possession of land or some other scarce resource that the other desires.

The history of white settlers' contacts with American Indians is, of course, well known, though only relatively recently has the Indian side of the story begun to be told.[6] It is composed of a continued series of white encroachments on Indian territories involving needless massacres (sometimes disguised as "battles") and broken treaties that, for the most part, involved contests over land. What may not be as well known to American students is that similar conflicts between white settlers and native peoples have occurred throughout many other parts of the world, especially in Australia, New Zealand, Canada, and Africa.[7] In all these situations, since the native groups were initially in possession of land desired by the invading settlers (who depicted themselves as "discovering" these territories), ways had to be found to deprive these initial landholders of their property.

In America this was done on a piecemeal basis by constantly driving diverse Indian tribes westward and onto smaller and smaller parcels of land that, at the time, were considered useless to whites. In the case of the Seminoles of Florida and the Cherokee Nation of Georgia and the Carolinas, it was accomplished by means of forced marches across the Mississippi, marches in which thousands perished. In other instances Indians were either slaughtered or decimated by disease. In still others, Indians were "given" parcels of land through a series of treaties that remained in effect only until the land they had been assigned became valuable to a new group of white settlers. Much the same pattern has occurred in other regions of the world, with the exception that in some cases—for example the Tasmanians of Australia and the Hotentot and Bushmen tribes of South Africa—the original native groups have totally disappeared.

Each of these histories shares a common characteristic: competition over land was direct and clearly defined along group lines, because the weaker, original inhabiting group could only be deprived of this land through a combination of force and deception. In effect, there was no competition at all, since the odds were so uneven. To the extent there was competition, however, it took the form of a considerable amount of *instrumental aggression*—that is, behaviors that were intended to injure the other party *also* helped to assure settlers that they would be able to displace these native groups from whatever lands they desired at the time. Such aggression was in many instances returned in the form of retaliatory raids, leading to extensive conflict that resulted in the decimation of the weaker groups.

Thus this particular means of competition for land almost universally led to aggression and conflict between organized groups, rather than among individuals. Such organized conflict over territory has, of course, existed throughout recorded history and is by no means peculiar to conflict among racial or ethnic groups. In the case of the expansion of European colonial powers in the last two centuries, however, there were much more extensive contacts between peoples with extremely different cultural and biological heritages, so that the ethnic and racial "badges" were far more significant in the minds of parties in mutual contact.

There are other situations in which intergroup competition is fostered by the rather sudden intrusion of a very distinct group, often in a setting where an undersupply of desired objectives exists, whether this be land, food supplies, or jobs.[8] We noted earlier that various European ethnic groups immigrated to America in waves, each time competing for jobs with those who occupied slightly more favored positions in the economy. Usually such groups were seen as undercutting the bargaining position of this existing labor force by leading to a reduction in wages, by creating a large supply of unemployed workers, or by serving as strike-breakers. Again, this has become a common phenomenon throughout the modern world, but it has been intensified as a result of improved transportation facilities, active labor recruitment processes, and extensive communication networks that make it possible for large numbers of persons to learn about opportunities elsewhere.

We have already noted that Chinese immigrants to the United States faced extreme hostility once their labor was no longer needed and they began to compete for jobs in the mines and in urban areas along the Pacific coast. A similar situation also faced many of the white immigrant groups on the East coast, so much so that the restrictive immigration laws of the 1920s were only slightly less effective in cutting off this source of cheap labor than the Chinese restriction laws of the previous century. More recently, Puerto Rican immigrants to New York City and other Northeastern cities, Cuban exiles in Miami, and Chicano migrants to Los Angeles, San Diego, and other Southwestern cities have also encountered the same problems. In all these instances a readily identified group has rather dramatically "intruded" into job markets where their competitive position has been resented and where, as a result, this competition became defined along ethnic lines instead of being seen as a problem of unrelated individuals. When Vietnamese and Cuban refugees, who have been admitted to this country in large numbers, settle in a few areas that are undergoing an economic recession, we are not surprised to see much the same reaction.[9]

RESENTMENT OF MINORITY SUCCESS

Some minorities carry with them into a competitive situation certain special advantages that Wagley and Harris have referred to as an "adaptive capacity."[10] To the extent that such minorities specialize and occupy particular occupational niches where they are both highly visible and also successful, we can expect that competition will be defined along group lines and that hostility toward these minorities will mount. We have already noted that certain minorities throughout the world may be characterized as middle-class minorities that are economically better off than many others with whom they are in potential competition. Sometimes such minorities disperse themselves within the economy, both geographically and in terms of the occupations they hold. But initially there is apt to be a rather long and sometimes tense period in which they come to occupy a specific occupational niche that is dependent upon their ability to transmit a specific set of skills to succeeding generations. This niche may even be occupied over a number of centuries, depending on the rapidity with which the economy is itself undergoing basic changes.

Jews in America represent a middle-class minority that is becoming reasonably dispersed occupationally, and the same appears to be occurring among Japanese-Americans. Chinese-Americans, however, still tend to be ghettoized to a greater extent and are also heavily concentrated in certain types of occupations that are highly associated with these spatially segregated communities. The "Chinatowns" of San Francisco and other major cities immediately come to mind, as do Chinese restaurants and small retail outlets. As already noted, Chinese populations in South Asia have likewise concentrated in urban areas and have entered many of the same kinds of occupations that European Jews occupied for centuries—small businesses, peddling, moneylending, and positions as petty officials.[11] During the period of colonial expansion into the Asian continent, Eurasians, capitalizing on their mixed parentage and marginal cultural position, found themselves in a strong competitive position to occupy the lower and intermediate rungs of government and European-controlled business enterprises. Many Indians and Asians occupied similar positions in Africa, even in South Africa where whites were present in larger numbers.

Whenever a middle-class minority does occupy these special occupational niches, there is a double reason why they are likely to be singled out for hostility and scapegoating. First, while they are successful, they are also vulnerable, since they rarely have the political power to accompany their favorable economic position. Usually small in number—except in the case of major commercial cities such as Singapore or Bangkok—such minorities are convenient to political elites in times of prosperity by virtue of their important contributions to the market economy.[12] But in times of scarcity and political unrest they become ideal scapegoats who serve to deflect hostility away from these political elites.

Secondly, minorities who occupy these middle-class jobs are themselves sources of frustration to the populations with which they must deal. As small-time merchants, moneylenders, tax collectors, or petty officials they play a middleman role that is highly visible and irritating to those who purchase their goods (at prices that are perceived to be too high), who take out loans (at high interest rates), or who deal with them as governmental representatives. Socialized into these middleman roles, members of these minorities often treat "outsiders" with a degree of impersonality and indifference that, though it may be functional to their role, is also highly irritating. They are thus easily stereotyped in the fashion we described earlier—as being unethical, grasping, overly ambitious, and in general willing to violate the many norms that have been developed to regulate interaction among members of the dominant group. They are seen as strangers in one's midst, as agents of hated but invulnerable elites, and as being willing to do almost anything for a quick profit.

Periodic crises or depressions, during which they serve as convenient scapegoats, may lock such minorities into these middleman positions for a very long period: just as tensions begin to subside, as the minority begins to adopt less "foreign" ways and to disperse itself through the economy, a new crisis arises for which it is blamed, forcing its members to retreat inward, to reduce contacts with members of the "host" community, and to transmit to the next generation those very same proven skills that are highly successful competitively but also a source of friction between themselves and the majority.

In this respect the long history of Jews in medieval Europe is fairly similar to that of the Chinese in South Asia. The experience of the largely ethnic-Chinese "boat people" currently being forced out of Vietnam in many ways also parallels that of the millions of Jews who were expelled from Russia and Eastern Europe a half-century to a century ago. Like them, Chinese possessions and businesses are being conveniently "appropriated" to the advantage of the ethnic majorities who have envied their position. Mentioned earlier, the same phenomenon occurred in this country in 1942 when Japanese-Americans were placed in "detention centers" and their landholdings and businesses taken away.

PATTERNS OF MINORITY SIZE, CONCENTRATION, AND SOCIAL VISIBILITY

If a minority is extremely small in comparison with the majority population it is not likely to be noticed unless its behaviors are particularly offensive to that majority. Most likely, its members will be treated with curiosity and perhaps a slight disdain that will probably disappear once the members are recognized as individuals whose unique characteristics are no longer obscured by a few conspicuous traits such as skin color, dress, or mannerisms. If the minority does not require special treatment and is not handicapped by, say, a lack of understanding of the local language or customs, it is likely that it will soon disappear as a minority "problem," even if there is little or no intermarriage with members of the larger population.

There is of course no exact tipping point at which a minority's size is likely to bring about a stronger reaction, as this will depend on such things as its racial distinctiveness, the degree to which its behavior violates local norms, the extent to which it voluntarily segregates itself, and the nature of the local competitive arena. Since all social systems are in mutual contact to varying degrees, there will also undoubtedly be a number of *exogenous* or outside factors that are involved, inluding whatever minority stereotypes are in evidence in this outside environment. Perhaps the crucial minority percentage is somewhere around five to ten percent, but any such figure is only a rough estimate. A minority of this approximate size becomes not only visible as a distinct group, but, if there is a situation of labor surplus, several occupations will likely be disproportionately occupied by the minority to the detriment of a significant segment of the majority labor force.

In these instances the dominant group's fear of economic competition can motivate discrimination, aggression, or attempts at expulsion against visible minorities. Economic security is obviously an almost universally high priority (utility) in actors' goal hierarchies, but there will be occasions—especially during periods of rapid change—when subjective probabilities of achieving these goals by "legitimate" means will be either very low or extremely difficult to calculate. Thus, excluding or otherwise controlling a minority will often be *perceived* as an effective means of regulating competition, whether or not this is actually the case.

The isolated individual will rarely be in a position to deal with a minority in this manner, but an organized effort can very well succeed provided the minority is not too large and is not in a position to rely on the support of other parties, such as governmental officials or local employers. Employers especially may waver between enforcing the law, taking a stance favoring the minority, or remaining conveniently inactive. If they, themselves, stand a risk of becoming an additional scapegoat they are especially likely to refrain from serving as the minority protector.

Minorities of relatively small size are thus especially likely to be in an insecure position. They are large enough to be noticed (and sometimes welcomed in times of labor scarcity), but they may also serve as very convenient scapegoats in times of crisis. Both visible and vulnerable, they make plausible targets of blame for economic frustrations such as a shortage of jobs.

Minorities of substantial size constitute both a political threat to the dominant group and a potentially useful coalition partner. Depending on circumstances, they may be treated with either considerable respect or hostility, but they are rarely treated with indifference. In the *Strange Career of Jim Crow*, the noted historian C. Vann Woodward documented the vacillation of the Populist Party in the South during the 1890s, a time when major efforts were being made to wrest political control from the hands of conservatives.[13] At first Populist leaders such as the notorious Tom Watson actively solicited the votes of blacks. At this time, blacks were characterized as fellow victims of conservative policies who, along with their white brethren, were urged to unite to create a Populist majority. But once it became apparent that the black vote was both divided and disappointingly small, these very same Populist leaders, Watson included, turned their full fury onto the helpless blacks. The result was one of the most extreme periods in American history in terms of violations of civil rights. A whole series of restrictive "Jim Crow" laws were passed that went far beyond the goal of regulating economic competition or making it impossible for blacks to vote in Southern elections. They virtually assured the complete segregation of the races.

In some cases it has been the *dominant group* that has been a nation's minority population. Today there is only one major country remaining in which a numerically smaller white population has *both* economic and political control over a much larger black population, namely the Union of South Africa. As recently as 1979, however, Rhodesia (now Zimbabwe) was also in this category. In both countries anti-black measures were extreme and potential violence never far beneath the surface. Obviously, whenever the dominant party is also a numerical minority, a number of very strict control measures must be applied.

In South Africa a host of such restrictive laws have been passed. These laws regulate the physical movements of blacks, make political protest a seditious act, restrict the legal rights of blacks and their allies, regulate job competition, and create as much spatial separation between the races as is compatible with economic efficiency. Known as *Apartheid*, this official South African "theory" envisages virtually total racial separation, with "Natives" being confined to special reserves, which of course are located on marginal lands and are far too small to permit more than a bare subsistence economy. But since native labor is needed throughout the economy, total Apartheid was never really put into practice. Instead, the black population of South Africa exists in a kind of limbo—supposedly settled within its own enclaves but, in fact, permitted to live and work at the convenience of the white-controlled government.

One last, and very extreme, numerical relationship can be noted in passing, since the pattern in question is now only of historical interest. In the case of a few colonial territories, the number of whites living in them has been so small—sometimes less than one percent—that no major economic stakes for individual settlers were ever really at issue.[14] Several British colonies in West Africa, as well as the Belgian Congo, had such severe climatic disadvantages (for whites) that they were administered by a tiny group of governmental officials and company managers. Most of these persons were rotated within the colonial territories on a short-term basis. The colonial powers also found it necessary to fill the lower- and middle-level bureaucratic positions with "Westernized" natives. No politically important white settler groups existed in these territories, with the result that once the colonial era ended after World War II, these territories were simply given over to the native populations with little or no resistance on the part of local whites. In effect, the percentage of members of the dominant group was *so* small that it would have been out of the question to attempt a white-controlled minority government. Those whites who remained did so at the invitation of the newly formed governments.

OCCUPATIONAL CONTROLS ON INTERGROUP COMPETITION

Whether occupational competition is defined along individualistic lines or in terms of intergroup relations will also depend upon a number of other features that affect the degree to which actors organize cooperatively, either to restrict the position of some other group of competitors or to bargain for a larger total slice of the pie. For instance, if actors are geographically spread apart and are only seldom in communication with one another, in this setting we would naturally expect the individualistic pattern to be more likely. This has certainly been most common, historically, with respect to farmers and peasant groups throughout the world, groups which can be contrasted with the occupational setting of, say, industrial laborers. It has also been more characteristic of female-dominated occupations, which until very recently have proved difficult for unions to organize. But it is also characteristic of a number of much more prestigious and high-paying professions.

This individualistic mode of competition is of course stressed in our American capitalist-oriented ideology. The "ideal" form of behavior, according to this philosophy, is oriented to success through hard work, careful preparation, saving, and long-range planning. One "gets ahead" by proving one's own worth through individual contributions to the benefit of the corporation or whatever other group is of concern. Accordingly, it is illegitimate to place roadblocks in the path of other potential competitors. In particular, discrimination against minorities—or other categories of persons—is considered harmful to the competitive system and to the welfare of the organization or state.

A very different ideological position is the notion that all workers should unite in a cooperative arrangement that sharply limits individualistic competition in favor of a common effort to bargain with the employer or other agent for a greater collective slice of the pie, and to protect the individual member against extreme competition. Here, competition is seen as a basic evil that is used in a power struggle between workers and management, or, as Marxists see it, between those who are producers of goods and services and those who appropriate the fruits of this labor for their own benefit.

In reality, we usually find various mixes of these two ideologies, a range of beliefs that usually coincide with each party's own vested interests. Most proffessions do in fact develop ways of limiting or regulating competition among members. They may restrict entry by regulating educational or apprenticeship programs. They may forbid advertising and competitive bidding among members. And they usually also develop codes of ethics which, among other things, have the function of keeping professional secrets or internal conflicts from becoming common knowledge among outsiders. In short, externally they will "close ranks" in the face of a potential threat, and internally they will attempt to assure members that competition does not get out of hand.

Labor unions use similar tactics. Here we need to distinguish between those unions that rely primarily on *exclusion* to control their numbers—for example, through tightly controlled apprenticeship programs—and those that depend upon large numbers of relatively unskilled laborers for effective bargaining. Craft unions involving skilled trades belong to the first category, whereas industrial unions (epitomized by the semiskilled assembly-line worker) represent the second. Although the latter type of union may attempt to exclude potential competitors from being hired in the first place—for example, through union contracts which require that previously hired union members be given back their old jobs before any others can be hired—once someone *is* hired, these unions basically must rely on numbers and undivided loyalties for bargaining power.

We see in these examples that a very common type of response to competition involves the cooperation among *some* persons to exclude *others* from the competitive race. The identity of these excluded "others" is often racial and ethnic.

There is, however, no inherent reason why the lines of exclusion cannot involve other categories of persons, as for example women, persons above or below certain ages, or newcomers to a community. All that is required is that the competitors have the necessary resources and opportunities for organization to accomplish the exclusion. Often, of course, they do not. This can be illustrated with an example from professional sports.

Consider the case of professional baseball, which blacks have entered in substantial numbers ever since Jackie Robinson became a member of the Brooklyn Dodgers in 1947. These athletes are highly paid and enjoy considerable prestige and publicity. But they must compete *strictly as individuals*, and careers in most cases are hazardous and brief. Performance levels are extremely easy to evaluate and competition among employers for the best talent is intense and highly organized. Furthermore, the very large nationwide network of training programs and "feeder" teams makes it virtually impossible to block the path of a promising young athlete. Thus, since there was already a large pool of talented black players available to enter the major leagues, once the initial racial barrier had been broken professional baseball became wide open to minorities, with other professional sports soon to follow.

Contrast that situation with many other occupations that can be tightly controlled through apprenticeship or technical training programs, entry into which is determined by a small number of "gatekeepers" of the dominant race or ethnic group. The building trades are an excellent example of this type of occupation, as are many professional groups such as doctors, dentists, and lawyers. Until recently, all of these occupations contained only a tiny number of minority members, and it was not until governmental affirmative-action programs were put into effect that the scramble began to find qualified minority (and women) applicants. Representatives of these occupations vigorously deny that discrimination has ever been intended, their argument usually being that very few minority (or women) candidates have applied for admission to these programs. Although this has indeed sometimes been the case, it is due in large part to a "self-fulfilling prophesy" phenomenon: minorities have not *believed* that they would be accepted and therefore have often not obtained the necessary prerequisite training. Since few then applied, and even fewer were admitted, the occupations then became identified as exclusively white or male.

One American minority *has* attempted to enter these restrictive occupations, however: namely Jews. Once strict quotas were used to regulate the number of Jews admitted into the prestigious colleges and medical and law schools. When this practice was exposed following World War II, a more subtle one of territorial quotas was instituted. Since Jews were heavily concentrated in New York City and a few other Eastern cities, it was possible to restrict their numbers by simply reducing the proportions admitted from these areas and arguing in favor of "regional diversity." This is one reason why many members of the Jewish minority are deeply suspicious of any quota system, even where it favors a minority. They have experienced these quotas first hand and recognize that quotas can easily be used to hinder minorities as well as assist them.

Historically, the relationship between American labor unions and blacks and other lower-class minorities has been a mixed one because of the fact that certain types of unions—mainly the craft or skilled trades—must rely on the device of restricting membership in order to control their numbers, whereas others, as for example auto and steel workers, longshoremen, and teamsters must rely heavily on their ability to gain the loyalty of numerous potential strike-breakers. When the latter unions have been strong, and their power consolidated, majority and minority workers usually find themselves on the same side, working in mutual cooperation. But when these unions have been weak and have had to rely on force and intimidation to control competitors, racial and ethnic conflict has often been intense. Anti-Irish and anti-Catholic labor movements during the previous century, along with anti-Asian movements, have given way to anti-black movements during the past fifty to one hundred years. If rates of unemployment begin to rise during the next decade, and if immigration from Mexico continues to be substantial, we may expect hostility toward this ethnic group to increase as well.

INTIMIDATION AND CULTURAL
INHIBITION AS MINORITY-CONTROL MECHANISMS

The existence of organizations such as the Ku Klux Klan, as well as the extremely high lynching rates that existed within the South for the approximately 50 years between 1880 and 1930, are in part explainable as attempts to control minority competition by a different type of device. Lacking the *economic* means to control this minority competition, and also lacking the organization of an industrial union capable of bargaining through strength of numbers, working-class whites found it much simpler to control blacks through the technique of intimidation and violence. Prior to World War II, and even afterwards, an industrious black in many parts of the South did not *dare* to appear too prosperous. Otherwise, he or she would be defined as "uppity" and might be marked for violent treatment. It is no wonder, then, that blacks failed to apply for good jobs.

Equally significant in the long run, Southern blacks found it necessary to develop a number of protective mechanisms to assure white competitors that they knew their proper "place." These included displays of deferential behavior, strong inhibitions against fighting back or in any way appearing insolent or unappreciative, and the necessity of maintaining a social "mask" for whites that was consistent with the stereotype of blacks as happy, childlike, and basically rather stupid people. Such socialization patterns not only created severe problems of lowered self-esteem, but they also reinforced patterns of in-group self-hatred. Black violence, for example, was turned inward toward members of their own group. High murder rates within the black community were tolerated, if not actually encouraged, by a legal system that basically defined intra-black aggression as not only inconsequential but also "natural."[15]

Taking the law into one's own hands is especially likely whenever the strictly *economic* bargaining power of dominant-group individuals is weak and where official governmental policies are at least in theory protective of the minority. An interesting variant on this theme has been played out in those colonial territories that were occupied by the Catholic nations of Spain and Portugal. The Church and the monarchies in these two countries in effect formed a coalition against those settlers who attempted to rise in the social order by taking advantage of the local native population (or, in the case of Brazil, who imported black slaves).[16] *Official* policies and pronouncements were reasonably protective of these minorities, but unfortunately both Church and state authority were weak compared to the power of local whites who had immediate economic stakes and who could easily get by with various forms of quasi-legal or illegal aggression. A somewhat similar pattern also occurred in the case of American Indian tribes who, for the most part, found themselves at the mercy of local settlers, traders, and army personnel regardless of what the treaties they signed may have said.

Where a government can actually be controlled by the interests of dominant-group members who wish to restrict minority competition, the result is more likely to be a set of *laws* that operate to regulate this competition without the use of violence or threats of violence. We have already noted the case of South Africa, where a whole series of laws have been passed that confine native workers to specific residential areas, regulate wages that can be paid to them, and force them to carry special "passes" that have the net effect of closely regulating their physical movements. These laws are reinforced by a system of justice that makes it possible for persons to be imprisoned, without trial, for prolonged periods of time for extremely vague offenses.

The simple belief that persons who find themselves in a common competitive situation will unite to work toward their common betterment—if only they can be made to see the wisdom of this strategy—is thus a very naive one at best. It fails to take into consideration that cooperation among a segment of such a population may lead to intense *intergroup* competition, as well as the use of means that in our own society are considered "illegitimate." These include devices to restrict entry into an occupation, violence and intimidation, and political actions resulting in legalized sanctions that have the same purpose.

Whereas some individuals in a competitive situation will make choices in accord with ethical, religious, or other culturally prescribed principles, many others will attempt solutions that seem to them most expedient given whatever resources or competitive advantages they may have. Whether or not they succeed will depend on a variety of factors, including variables relating to the nature of the occupation or competitive arena, the relative size of the minority, policies of third parties that may affect the balance of power, and, of course, the way that the minority itself reacts.

IMPERSONAL FACTORS AFFECTING COMPETITIVE RESOURCES

The competitive position of a minority—or, for that matter, any other category of individuals—can be affected by a large number of social and economic factors that only incidentally involve prejudice or discrimination. It is therefore important for a minority to adjust its behavior by taking these factors into consideration, if at all possible. Changes in technology often will have profound effects on an economy, and a minority may or may not be in a position to adapt to these changes. Sometimes it will be prevented from doing so, perhaps by the device of withholding needed resources or educational skills. But the minority *itself* may retard its own adaptation if it attempts to react to changes by rigidly hanging onto past practices or traditions that handicap this adjustment. If the changes are gradual enough to go unnoticed, the minority may find its competitive position eroded without becoming aware of what has taken place.

As previously noted, minorities differ with respect to what Wagley and Harris called their "adaptive capacities," or what, in another work, the author has referred to as their "competitive resources."[17] Given the reality of an ever-changing world, *all* human groups must find ways of maintaining their competitive positions—even though they may react negatively to these changes, say, by attempting a withdrawal strategy of the type that will be discussed in Chapter 6 —or they will lose out. Many so-called "nativistic movements" have had this characteristic, namely, a self-conscious attempt to reconstruct an idealized past or to locate a semiisolated position in a larger economy.

Universally, all groups will find themselves undergoing strains in the face of change, as some members attempt to direct energies toward adapting whereas others pull in the opposite direction. But racial and ethnic groups usually find themselves under even greater strains because of their subordinate positions and their dependence on the policies of groups over which they have little control. The impacts on minority individuals are also often extreme, and this is especially the case with respect to members of so-called "marginal" minorities with orientations toward distinct subcultures. Detribalized American Indians are an obvious case in point.

Although we cannot study them in detail in this short work, it is necessary to outline a few of the major trends in the United States that have affected the competitive positions of our important minorities. First, there has been a continuous movement out of agricultural occupations, as well as a marked reduction in the relative importance of the small family farm as compared to that of the huge industrial farm.

Second, there is a diminishing demand for unskilled labor, including work that requires considerable physical strength or endurance or that is highly dangerous. Automation of industry and the increase in the service sector, together with the above-mentioned reduction in farm labor, has led to a considerable relative increase in white-collar occupations, particularly professionals and managerial personnel.

Third, the percentage of women engaged in part-time or full-time work outside the home has also increased rather steadily over the past several decades, to the point where about half of all working age women are currently in the labor force. Official estimates are misleading in one major respect. Although women have always been in the "labor force" as broadly defined to include farming and homemaking, today they are increasingly seeking paid jobs in competition with both white and minority males. Given that there is a decreasing demand for labor requiring physical strength, as well as a decline in the proportion of dangerous occupations, white women find themselves in a very favorable position in relation to minority males. This is especially true in industries where women employees have proven themselves more resistant to unionization and more willing to accept lower pay for work, which some may consider as merely supplemental or temporary income for the family budget. In effect, many white women are in direct competition with minorities, with both groups being paid wages and salaries that would not be acceptable to white males.

Fourth, there has been an overall *urbanward* movement, which in the case of lower-class minorities has involved a piling up within the central cities of our largest metropolitan areas. Some of these cities are now approaching an actual majority of minority residents. In 1970 blacks constituted 71 percent of the population in Washington, D.C., 46 percent in Baltimore, 33 percent in Chicago, 44 percent in Detroit, and 41 percent in St. Louis. [18] Yet at the same time, many of our industries are moving *outward* from central cities to suburban districts, where land and taxes are much cheaper, parking space is more available, and employees more satisfied. (Specialized professional services and banking centers tend to remain more centrally located, however.) Thus, paradoxically, professional personnel—who are overwhelmingly white and who live in the suburbs—are employed in the very same urban areas where minorities tend to live, whereas employment opportunities for blue-collar workers are increasingly found in the suburbs. This pattern in itself places many minority workers at a severe handicap.[19]

Finally, immigration patterns have an obvious impact on the competitive position of all those whose skill levels are approximately the same as those of the immigrant populations. We have already noted that the manipulation of immigrant quotas is one device through which employers may undercut the competitive position of local workers by flooding their industry with eager newcomers. It has often been *labor* movements—sometimes supposedly "radical" ones—that have been in the forefront in forcing the passage of restrictive immigration policies, as was the case in the 1880s with quota restrictions on the Chinese and in the 1920s with the Japanese and East European minorities.[20] Today, American-dwelling Chicanos are divided on the question of Mexican immigration (though they are in general agreement in resenting the stigma attached to the so-called "wetback," as well as fearing that controls applied to illegal immigrants are likely to spill over to themselves). Here it must be emphasized that much immigration, as well as the large-scale migration from Puerto Rico to New York and other Eastern cities, stems primarily from population pressures and economic poverty in regions elsewhere in the world.

Many of these same patterns relating to industrialization can be found throughout the world. Given that most developing nations are falling substantially behind the industrialized nations in competitive resources, and that their economies are still in large part dominated by a world economy controlled by the industrial powers, we find them experiencing severe problems of urbanward migration coupled with hidden unemployment or underemployment. It is a historical accident that most of the people in these developing nations are also non-white, but we are now in the unfortunate position where racial differences have been *labeled* as or are *believed* to be important factors accounting for their economic problems, or what, during the era of colonial expansionism, were taken to be their "backward"cultures. Thus race and ethnicity have become hopelessly confounded with issues that are predominantly economic and political, so that whiteness and dominance are seen as going hand in hand.

In the case of many "native" peoples throughout the world, as well as within our own country, economic techniques that were at one time adaptive and reasonably efficient are no longer competitive in comparison with mechanized ones. For example, consider the plight of small Eskimo tribes competing with huge Russian and Japanese whaling fleets, or contrast the very unequal resources of Indian salmon fishermen with those of white commercial fishermen. The dilemma is especially severe for a minority that is attempting to revitalize itself by teaching its younger generation a respect for past ways, including traditional labor techniques that are far less efficient than those used by their successful competitors. Northwest Coast Indians, who rely partly on traditional fishing methods, have had to employ noneconomic means—including the enforcement of treaty obligations—to assure themselves of a fixed quota of salmon. In the mid 1970s small Washington-state tribes won a series of court rulings that awarded them 50 percent of the salmon catch, clearly a substantial economic victory that, if consolidated, will provide them with an excellent source of livelihood. White commercial fishermen, however, have vigorously protested this Indian victory, with the result that legislative action to abrogate these treaties has been threatened. If the Indians subsequently lose this treaty right, it will of course not be the first time treaties made with the U.S. Government have not been honored.

A similar sort of competitive disadvantage has been noted in the case of minority businesses, which are nearly always quite small in comparison with white-owned ones.[21] Perhaps fifty years ago such small businesses might have been competitive and have developed into modest sized ones today. But it is now practically impossible for *any* small business—except in a few minor service-oriented areas such as beauty parlors or funeral homes—to compete effectively in a market that is primarily oriented to mass-produced goods. We are all aware that small food stores charge more than supermarkets and that discount houses offer substantial savings as compared with local hardware or clothing stores. Even the local restaurant has a hard time competing with fast-food chains, which is only to say that even the nature of retail business has changed, to say nothing of manufacturing or wholesale enterprises. Minority members, like everyone else, are becoming employees and managers, rather than owners. If they cannot adapt to these changes—or if they are prevented by discrimination from doing so—then they will be at a severe competitive disadvantage.

In large part as a result of the Civil Rights movement of the 1960s, as well as the Women's Rights movement, the United States government and a number of state and municipal governments have enacted and enforced numerous "affirmative action" programs designed to give selected minorities and women certain advantages in the competitive process. In many instances these programs have required private employers, unions, and government departments to adopt very specific plans or "goals" for increasing their minority or female employment percentages. Opponents of these programs have argued, in effect, that such goals amount to rigid quotas and to what they term "reverse discrimination" against whites and males.

Principles of equity are very much in dispute in these instances. On the one hand, minorities (and women) point to long histories of blatant discrimination, to the need for compensatory programs to assure that employers will not continue to practice such discrimination surreptitiously, and to the importance of minority role models to provide incentives for younger persons to obtain the necessary training for these positions. On the other hand, many white males—especially from among white ethnic groups that have not been singled out for favored treatment—claim that affirmative-action quotas are not only unfair to them as individuals but that they often result in far less-qualified individuals filling important jobs. At the present time, it is difficult to predict how this issue of affirmative action will turn out, though it seems it is being accepted with grudging reluctance, except by those who are most immediately affected. Obviously, as already implied, quotas are a two-edged sword, and their approval often depends upon whose vested interests are being affected.

Inequality, which will concern us in the next chapter, essentially results from a *combination* of actual discriminatory treatment of minorities and of minority responses to that discrimination. In addition, as we have just emphasized, inequality also results from impersonal economic forces that affect the competitive positions of many various groups in any society. It becomes essential, then, to try to assess the relative importance of each cause of inequality and then to develop long-range policies to reduce these inequalities. An understanding of similarities and differences among minorities and across social settings is therefore a crucial element for any future resolutions of this important societal problem.

NOTES

1. See Edna Bonacich, "A Theory of Ethnic Antagonism: The Split Labor Market," *American Sociological Review*, 37 (1972), pp. 547–59; see also, Edna Bonacich, "Advanced Capitalism and Black/White Race Relations in the United States: A Split Labor Market Interpretation," *American Sociological Review*, 41 (1976), pp. 34–51.

2. One of the earlier classics on the exploitative situation in South Africa is I. D. MacCrone, *Race Attitudes in South Africa* (London: Oxford University Press, 1937). See also Eugene P. Dvorin, *Racial Separation in South Africa* (University of Chicago Press, 1952); Philip Mason, *Patterns of Dominance*, chaps. 9 and 10; and Edna Bonacich, "A Theory of Ethnic Antagonism."

3. See Stanford M. Lyman, *Chinese Americans* (New York: Random House, 1974), chap. 4; and Carey McWilliams, *Prejudice: Japanese-Americans: Symbol of Racial Intolerance* (Boston: Little, Brown, 1945), chap. 2.

4. The caste analogy was extensively applied to black-white relations in the South by the social anthropologist W. Lloyd Warner and his many students during the 1940s and was also utilized by Myrdal, *American Dilemma*, chap. 31. See especially John Dollard, *Caste and Class in a Southern Town*; Allison Davis and John Dollard, *Children of Bondage* (Washington: American Council on Education, 1940); and Allison Davis, B. B. Gardner, and M. R. Gardner, *Deep South* (University of Chicago Press, 1941). The notion of caste, as applied to the United States, was severely criticized by Oliver C. Cox in his book *Caste, Class, and Race* (New York: Doubleday, 1948).

5. For examples of theoretical discussions that build heavily on the theme of initial contacts see E. K. Francis, *Interethnic Relations*; E. Franklin Frazier, *Race and Culture Contacts in the Modern World* (New York: Knopf, 1957); and Stanley Lieberson, "A Societal Theory of Race and Ethnic Relations," *American Sociological Review*, 26 (1961), pp. 902–910.

6. See, for example, Dee Brown, *Bury My Heart at Wounded Knee* (New York: Holt, Rinehart and Winston, 1970); Vine Deloria, Jr., *Custer Died for Your Sins: An Indian Manifesto* (New York: Macmillan, 1969); and William T. Hagan, *American Indians* (University of Chicago Press, 1979).

7. See Grenfell Price, *White Settlers and Native Peoples* (Melbourne: Georgian House, 1950).

8. See Stanley Lieberson, "A Societal Theory of Race and Ethnic Relations;" and E. K. Francis, *Interethnic Relations*, especially chaps. 15 and 17.

9. According to news accounts in 1979, there have been several economic conflicts in small fishing towns in the United States that have involved relatively large groups of Vietnamese refugees. Whether these turn out to be isolated incidents remains to be seen.

10. Charles Wagley and Marvin Harris, *Minorities in the New World*, p. 239, pp. 264–73.

11. Stanford Lyman, *Chinese Americans*, chaps. 1 and 2, makes the point that this insulation of Chinese minorities in many parts of the world is reinforced by their very strong kinship organizations, combined with linguistic and territorial groups and secret societies, all of which crosscut each other in complex ways and that enable Chinese minorities to resist acculturation to the local societies.

12. Hannah Arendt, in her classic work *The Origins of Totalitarianism* (New York: Harcourt Brace Jovanovich, Inc., 1973), develops the thesis that modern antisemitism in Germany and other parts of Western Europe did not really arise until Jews lost their economic *power*, while still retaining their wealth.

13. C. Vann Woodward, *The Strange Career of Jim Crow* (New York: Oxford University Press, 1957).

14. Philip Mason *(Patterns of Dominance)* suggests that the term "paternalistic" is much more appropriate for this type of race-relations situation than one in which there is much more obvious economic control, as for example under a system of slavery. This is in contrast with van den Berghe, *Race and Racism,* who uses the term in a much broader sense.

15. Although difficult to measure, it appears as though this tolerance of in-group aggression among blacks is gradually decreasing. Myrdal argued that it was quite extensive within the South prior to World War II. See Gunnar Myrdal, *An American Dilemma,* chaps. 24–26.

16. See Charles Wagley and Marvin Harris, *Minorities in the New World;* and Philip Mason, *Patterns of Dominance,* chaps. 11 and 13.

17. H. M. Blalock, *Toward a Theory of Minority-Group Relations,* chap. 4.

18. The percentages of black children in the public schools in these cities are much higher, indicating that mandatory busing within these cities must necessarily result in schools that are predominantly black. The percentages of blacks in the public elementary schools (1970) was as follows: Washington, D. C., 93 percent; Baltimore, 67; Detroit, 64; St. Louis, 65; and Chicago, 55. See Reynolds Farley, "Residential Segregation and Its Implications for School Integration," *Law and Contemporary Problems,* 39 (1975), pp. 164–93.

19. See Mark S. Granovetter, "The Strength of Weak Ties," *American Journal of Sociology,* 78 (1973), pp. 1360–80.

20. See Stanford Lyman, *Chinese Americans,* chap. 4; and Carey McWilliams, *Prejudice: Japanese-Americans,* chap. 2.

21. This point was strongly emphasized several decades ago by the black sociologist, E. Franklin Frazier in his works *The Negro in the United States,* chap. 16, and *Black Bourgoisie* (New York.: Free Press, 1957), chap. 7. More recently, Light has compared the relative success rates of black, Chinese- and Japanese-American business enterprises. See Ivan H. Light, *Ethnic Enterprise in America* (Berkeley: University of California Press, 1972).

CHAPTER 5
INEQUALITY, STATUS ATTAINMENT, AND EDUCATION

Problems relating to inequality have interested social philosophers for at least twenty-five hundred years and undoubtedly longer. They have also been the subject of considerable dispute among social scientists. Inequalities with respect to income, occupational roles, prestige, and power are clearly evident for all to see, and insofar as we are aware have existed in all human societies. Yet social systems do differ in several ways. For instance, they differ in terms of how positions and rewards are *allocated* to members. Do persons earn or achieve them or are they assigned on the basis of ascribed characteristics such as sex, race, family and kinship, or age? To what extent, for example, are occupations inherited or at least easily predicted by knowing the occupations of one's parents or kin?

There also are rather obvious differences in the overall *distributions* of valued goods or rewards. In some societies wealth and power are extremely concentrated in the hands of a few individuals and families, whereas the overwhelming majority are extremely poor or have virtually no power. Even among societies characterized by a continuous distribution of income or wealth, there may be considerable differences in degree of inequality. For instance, Lenski estimates that in the Soviet Union the ratio of the incomes of the top and bottom deciles is approximately three to one, whereas in our own country the comparable figure is approximately four times this large.[1] Although much more difficult to estimate, the dispersions in *power* within the two countries may be just the reverse, however.

In dealing with inequalities of any nature there are a number of crucial questions that must be asked. First, before one can talk scientifically one must be reasonably clear on the meaning of *inequality* and how it can be measured, at least ideally.[2] This subject, a complex one, we will sidestep by assuming that we are dealing with a reasonably simple notion such as that of income, wealth, or occupational prestige where we may use simple measures such as standard deviations or distances between top and bottom deciles or quartiles.[3] Much more difficult, however, is the problem of explaining why, in general, inequalities occur. So before addressing the limited question of accounting for inequalities within a given society, we must at least outline the essentials of three very different, recurrent explanations, ones which have been with us at least since the days of the early Greek philosophers.

The first explanation essentially holds that the individual is responsible for existing inequalities, arguing that, except for a few accidents of fate, most persons get what they deserve. That is, persons who are at or near the top of the social hierarchy are there because of a combination of hard work, ability, strong moral character, or adeptness in leading or persuading others. Conversely, those who are near the bottom have only themselves to blame. They are the least-skilled, most lazy, and least premeditating members of society and would find themselves in the same unfortunate position even if they were temporarily moved to the top.

We have already noted that many lower-class minorities are stereotyped in this fashion, but the essential point is that this type of explanatory model may be applied to any member of the lowest strata, regardless of race, creed, or color. Since virtually everyone knows of individuals whose behaviors fit one of these two models, this explanation always seems somewhat plausible. It is especially appealing to those near the top, and thus it becomes a cornerstone of many conservative ideologies.

A second explanation places much greater emphasis on a social system's properties or needs, in contrast with individualistic characteristics. This theory was stated well in a highly influential paper by Davis and Moore and has subsequently become known as the "functional" theory of stratification.[4] In simplest terms it holds that certain occupations or social roles are both functionally more important to the society than are others and also more difficult to fill because of the scarcity of persons having the necessary skills, training, or abilities to perform well in these positions. Since they are so important and also difficult to fill, a social system must find ways to reward the occupants of these positions. Thus persons in these roles will tend to receive higher income, be honored with recognition and status, and in many instances also be given power sufficient to assure that the system runs smoothly. In short, persons will be rewarded roughly in proportion to their contributions to the functioning of the social system. Although there may be some exceptions, the implication is that individuals will be allocated among positions in accord with performance standards, rather than in terms of ascribed characteristics such as sex, race, or family background. Deviations from such an achievement-oriented selective mechanism are considered "dysfunctional" to the system to the degree that they result in lowered efficiency in placing the best-qualified persons in the functionally most important positions.

A third general explanation for inequalities places a much greater emphasis on power. In its most extreme form the argument boils down to the thesis that actors will grab for themselves—and their closest relatives and friends—as large a slice of the pie as they can obtain, subject to restrictions placed upon them by others. Insofar as they are in positions to allocate rewards to others, they will do so not in terms of any functional importance to the *society* but, rather, in accord with their own interests, however they may define these to be.

According to Lenski, who develops a much more sophisticated line of argument in this connection, persons are assigned to positions primarily in accord with their expected contributions to those in positions of power, rather than to the society as a whole.[5] Thus the distribution of prestige and income, or other social rewards, will depend very heavily on the distribution of power in the social system. Gross inequalities, say in income, can thus result from the extreme concentration of power. Insofar as prestige or income can also be used as *sources* of power, they may also therefore feed back to perpetuate themselves.

Most of us will undoubtedly admit that there is a degree of plausibility to each of these theories, and there of course are additional explanations of inequality that include them in various combinations. If we are to move beyond ideological disputes, however, it becomes necessary to find ways of assessing the *degree* to which each kind of explanation accounts for any given system of inequality, say, with respect to income. This is an important though extremely difficult task that is obviously dependent on our obtaining adequate data. Furthermore, it must be attacked piecemeal by limiting ourselves to reasonably specific questions that can be answered by empirical means. In the next section we shall discuss one such mode of attack, which has been primarily limited to explaining income and occupational differences among individuals, rather than differences among societies. This approach also illustrates an area in which quantitative methods have been applied to sociological research.

STATUS-ATTAINMENT PROCESSES

Suppose we begin by asking what accounts for the differences among male incomes in U.S. society, thereby ruling out a host of problems concerning differences between male and female incomes, the relationship between income and accumulated wealth, or how incomes are related to living standards or family consumption patterns. Certainly, one major factor accounting for income differences will be one's occupation. But occupations may be categorized in a number of different ways, some of which lend themselves to quantification much more readily than others. One important method of scoring occupations is in terms of a type of prestige rating that was originally based on scores assigned to familiar occupations by respondents in national surveys. It was then found that, for such familiar occupations, prestige scores could be predicted very well by a combination of the average level of education of persons in these occupations, along with their median incomes.[6] It thus became possible to score a wide variety of oc-

cupations, including many that are not familiar to the general public. Occupations may, of course, be scored in other ways, as for example in terms of some
power dimension, and we shall comment on this matter below. For the time
being, however, let us assume that incomes can be partly explained in terms of
occupational prestige.

We next ask, How do males in our society come to be assigned to occupations? In part, it is clearly a matter of self-selection, as well as "accident." But
we know that their formal educations also have a great deal to do with their
allocation to occupations. One very simple measure of "education" is the number of years of formal schooling. Although we also recognize that all college or
high-school graduates are not alike with respect to school quality, type of program, ability, or amount of occupationally relevant information they possess, let
us for the moment confine ourselves to years of schooling, however.

Adding in income difference itself, we now have three variables: income,
occupational prestige, and years of schooling. How do these fit together causally?
We assume that education in most instances ceases prior to job entry and that
one's income cannot possibly affect one's earlier education. It seems plausible to
try out a simple causal model, as indicated in Figure 1, in which education serves
as a direct cause of income, as well as an indirect one through occupational
prestige. By "direct cause" we mean direct *relative* to the other variables in the
diagram. Thus in this illustration there may be certain unspecified mechanisms
through which education can affect income, in ways other than through the
nature of one's occupation. One of these mechanisms may be through knowledge or ability, which is not measured or explicitly considered in the model.
"Directness" of causation is thus a relative notion, depending on the variables we
have explicitly included in the model.[7]

Such a three-variable model is obviously oversimplified. Let us then consider what additional factors might affect a person's educational level. Here we
may wish to bring in his intelligence or ability level, say, as indicated by a bat-
tery of I.Q. tests or perhaps a set of performance measures. Presumably, intelligence (or performance levels on tests) may have been taken into consideration
by whomever has decided to hire the person, so that we may draw in a direct

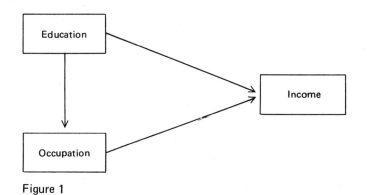

Figure 1

arrow from intelligence to occupation. Such intelligence may also carry over to job performance, as we would expect, so that it may "directly" affect one's income (assuming occupation has been controlled). Thus there is an additional arrow between intelligence and income, as indicated in the model of Figure 2.

How is intelligence (or performance level) affected by early socialization? Do any of the variables that affect socialization also directly affect the nature of one's occupation? Perhaps sons of professionals are not only given advantages within the home but are also given a special break in terms of a favored position at the point of job entry. If we use the variables "father's education" and "father's occupation" as surrogates for this host of socialization variables, then perhaps we will be willing to allow for direct links between these variables and both years of education and the occupational prestige of the son. We may assume, however, that the impacts of father's education and occupation on income are only indirect, through the intervening variables of intelligence, education, and occupational prestige. If so, we would omit the direct arrows between father's education and occupation and son's income, though it is possible to *test* for this assumption provided that adequate data are available.[8] These added complications have been built into the somewhat more complete model of Figure 3.

Perhaps we have gone far enough to make the point that causal models of this sort can become highly complex. For instance, in the "classic" study in this field that has spawned a host of alternative models, Blau and Duncan inserted "first occupation" into the model and visualized the process in terms of a sequence of job moves in which one's first occupation will obviously influence later occupational choices, as well as future incomes.[9] Were we to compare men and women, blacks and whites, or different age groupings, we would also find important differences that could be incorporated into the models. For instance, sex may have little to do with years of schooling but may very well affect the

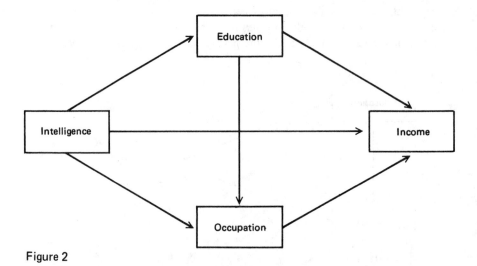

Figure 2

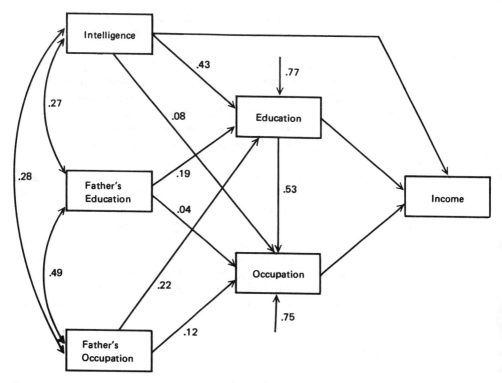

Figure 3

nature of the fields studied, and of course this latter variable has not been included in any of our figures. There may be rather large sex differences in terms of specific occupations selected. Female-dominated occupations may command much lower incomes, on the average, even where prestige and skill level are controlled. Many of these relationships have, in fact, been found in the empirical literature, but it would take us too far afield to consider them here.

Before turning to a number of specific findings of research based on causal analyses of this type, it is important to note that arrows representing "direct" effects of one variable on another have differing amounts of impact. Strength of relationship varies by degree, and so it is important to attach numerical values that in effect weigh each variable's relative importance. Suppose we wish to compare the relative contributions of intelligence and father's education on a person's own education. We immediately encounter a problem owing to the fact that schooling is measured in terms of years, whereas intelligence will be measured in terms of test scores. We therefore need to make these units comparable by standardizing the variables in some fashion. These standardized measures, which are obtained by dividing each variable by its standard deviation, are referred to as "path coefficients."[10] They tell us how a standard-deviation unit change in a given variable, controlling for the other causes, would impact upon the dependent variable in terms of its own standard-deviation units. Thus differences in father's education or intelligence are made comparable with one another in terms of whatever dispersions they may have within the sample being investigated.

Some of these numerical values have been inserted into Figure 3 and are based on data provided by Duncan, Featherman, and Duncan.[11] The numerical values that have been placed beside each arrow are standardized path coefficients that make it possible to compare the relative magnitudes of the direct effects of each variable. Ordinarily these coefficients have an upper limit of 1.0. It can be seen, for instance, that several of these direct effects are quite small, whereas two are substantial.

In Figure 3 we note a few additional conventions in this type of causal analysis. Curved double-headed arrows have been inserted to connect the three most causally early variables, for which we may wish to allow for empirical correlations among the variables without presuming anything about the reasons for these associations.[12] Notice also that there are small side-arrows, with accompanying numbers, directed from outside the causal system to each of the dependent variables, education and occupation. These remind us that our theoretical system is incomplete, and the sizes of the numerical coefficients associated with these side arrows give us measures of the unexplained variance in these two variables.[13]

Some Findings

One very important finding of studies in this area is that variables of this type by no means explain all of the variation in income or occupational prestige. This seems to imply that, unless measurement errors could account for much of this unexplained variation, there are probably many other factors responsible for these differences. Practically speaking, this suggests that incomes and occupations are certainly not "inherited," nor do racial or ethnic differences, themselves, come close to completely determining one's later statuses. This suggests, then, that American society is reasonably "open" in the sense that readily identifiable factors cannot reliably predict one's income or occupational prestige. Featherman and Hauser conclude, on the basis of a comparison of 1963 and 1973 data on males, that, if anything, a son's status is becoming slightly less predictable from his father's characteristics.[14] The father's characteristics appear to operate primarily on a son's educational levels, rather than having direct effects on either occupation or income. (See Figure 3 for one such set of results.)

Evidence suggests that there are at least a few differences between blacks and whites in the relative importance of the factors that link parental variables, such as education and occupation, to school performance and educational aspirations. Porter and also Kerckhoff and Campbell found that parental status variables have less impact on the educational aspirations of black youth than is the case with respect to their white counterparts, and Thomas has reported similar findings.[15] It has frequently been noted that black and white youth do not differ with respect to either their levels of self-respect or educational aspirations, however.[16] Kerckhoff and Campbell also found that mothers' characteristics are relatively more important in predicting blacks' aspiration levels than has been true for whites and that, for blacks, it is the *perception* of opportunities and the degree to which the individual believes that he or she has control over the environment that is the strongest predictor of aspiration levels.

Apparently, there is a stronger association between test performance and aspirations among whites than is the case for blacks, and also a stronger relationship between performance on standardized examinations and class rank in high school. Thus it may be that the mechanisms that motivate minority and dominant-group students may be somewhat different, at least with respect to the degree to which they affect aspirations, performance, and level of education attained. At this point, however, the findings are only suggestive with respect to precisely how these mechanisms operate.

Truly definitive data comparing several minorities are lacking, but as we have already noted, cultural differences can be expected to affect socialization patterns and, indirectly, such factors as school performance and levels of aspirations. Featherman and Hauser report that blacks have somewhat higher educational levels than Chicanos, as well as slightly higher returns from education in terms of occupational prestige.[17] If we control for father's status and the respondent's own education, however, Chicanos come out slightly ahead of blacks. Presumably, some of these slight differences are due to characteristics of the regions in which blacks and Chicanos are located, as well as the industrial characteristics of different urban areas.

The association between educational-achievement levels and one's later income is rather weak, at best, for all groups. Jencks and his associates argue on the basis of this finding that it makes little sense to worry about educational inequalities as predictors or as explanations for income inequalities.[18] They suggest, instead, that if one wishes to produce greater income equalities it makes much more sense, policy-wise, to attempt to modify the *income* distribution directly. For example, this might be achieved through progressive taxation policies that have the effect of redistributing incomes from the wealthy to the poor.

The relationship between occupational prestige and income is also rather modest, though in the predicted direction for all groups. In fact, the reader may recall that occupations are assigned prestige scores partly on the basis of *average* incomes. This does not imply, of course, that individuals who have the same occupational prestige necessarily have closely bunched incomes. In fact, there is some strong evidence that both women and minorities tend to find themselves in specific occupations that may have relatively higher prestige than income, whereas white males tend to cluster more into occupations that are simultaneously higher on both.[19]

This type of finding, along with the thesis that occupations need to be examined in terms of their relationship to the means of production, led Wright and Perrone to attempt to classify occupations in terms of their relative power, rather than their prestige.[20] Persons who are managers or officials of large corporations, as well as independent professionals such as doctors, lawyers, and dentists, are often in a position to extract higher salaries or fees than are persons in less powerful positions. Using this power dimension in addition to an occupation's prestige, Wright indeed found it possible to increase the explanatory power of this type of causal model. Given that most minorities (and white women) are very much underrepresented in these more powerful occupations, we would expect them to have smaller returns from their educations, even where occupational *prestige* has been controlled. Tendencies in this direction exist in the data, but one must be careful not to exaggerate the importance of this single mechanism. It does suggest, however, that serious efforts to include the power dimension in scoring occupations need to be made if we wish to achieve a more satisfactory causal explanation for income inequalities.

Predicting the occupations of black males is somewhat less reliable than is the case for whites.[21] Black sons begin with initial handicaps in terms of parental variables, which then affect their levels of educational achievements and therefore indirectly their occupational statuses and incomes. In the past decade or so blacks have been catching up rather rapidly in terms of educational levels attained by the younger age cohorts.[22] These relative gains in education are, in turn, yielding somewhat smaller relative gains in occupational prestige and income owing to blacks' lesser returns per added year of schooling (that is, blacks receiving fewer dollars per year of schooling than whites). The general processes linking education to occupation are similar for both races, however, and we presume that a corresponding pattern holds for Hispanics and other low-status minorities, though possibly with a decade or so lag in comparison with blacks.

Are these lesser returns to education on the part of minorities due to discrimination by employers? This is certainly one possible explanation for the fact that gains in education on the part of these minorities do not seem to have been matched by gains of the same magnitude in either occupational prestige or income. Here the picture is by no means clear. One alternative explanation, which is usually rejected by liberals, is that the *real* educational difference between groups has not been diminishing even though blacks and whites are becoming more similar with respect to *years* of formal schooling. For instance, performance on standardized exams (controlling for years of schooling) is known to differ by race, with blacks scoring below whites on both verbal and quantitative reasoning tests. If, for example, the average black high-school graduate performs at approximately the same level as the average ninth-grade white, then it might be argued that whites and blacks are not really being "equated" on true education. In effect, school quality and extent of actual learning are not being controlled.

The conclusions one reaches in this connection depend, then, on whether or not one is willing to accept the validity of such standardized tests as measures of "true" ability, knowledge, or whatever is of primary interest to employers.[23] We do know that blacks and Hispanics, on the average, score lower than whites, but we still cannot accurately assess how much of this difference is due to test bias and how much to true differences in learning or actual knowledge acquired. There is perhaps a clue in the fact that white women, too, experience less "payoff" for their education than do their male counterparts. Are there also sex differences in quality of education? This seems much less plausible, though we cannot completely rule out the possibility that sex differences with respect to income are due to such things as curriculum differences (for example fewer girls taking mathematics and science courses), or self-selection factors in choice of occupation. It seems very doubtful, however, that very much of the sex difference in incomes can be attributed to these factors. It seems much more likely that white women, along with minorities of both sexes, have been disadvantaged by discriminatory practices and their virtual exclusion from occupations that command sufficient power to extract high incomes. At least in this sense there seems to be substantial evidence that the "power" thesis of Lenski and others cannot easily be dismissed.

Another conclusion based on findings in the occupational-mobility literature is that, though upward intergenerational mobility (rising job status from father to son) has been reasonably extensive in American society, the *net* improvements in occupational status achieved by males in successive generations has been primarily due to changes in our occupational *structure*. That is, because there is less and less demand for farm laborers and unskilled workers and relatively more for white-collar workers and highly trained professionals, there has been a general drift upwards across generations, implying more upward than downward mobility.[24] This has been true for both whites and blacks, as well as other minorities, though as noted earlier this same trend may also be partly responsible for the relatively high unemployment rates among these minorities and others whose skill levels are below those now required in the labor market.

Has the momentum in minority gains begun to slacken since the end of the civil rights protests of the 1960s? Studies show no signs of such a slackening, but they also do not indicate cause for optimism that such inequalities will disappear within the forseeable future.[25] Though projections over more than a decade are risky, various extrapolations of recent trends suggest that it will be at least fifty to a hundred years before black-white differentials will become insignificant. Many factors may intervene to change these trends during the interim, of course.

Two additional findings with respect to trends are perhaps worth reporting. Featherman and Hauser have found tendencies for job mobility patterns among young blacks to be more predictable, and presumably more regularized, than is the case for somewhat older black cohorts.[26] Their findings pertain to males only, however. It has also been found that although the income inequalities between white and black males are being reduced (and also for females), this is not the case with respect to *family* income inequalities. The number of female-headed households among both whites and blacks has been increasing at a high rate, but relatively more so for blacks.[27] Since women's incomes are substantially below those of men's, the much larger percentage of black female-headed families has, in effect, cancelled out the relative gains for black individuals.[28]

Present data pertain to intervals prior to 1975, at which time the implications of the worldwide oil shortage and double-digit inflation had not become apparent to the American public. As political pressures mount to reduce welfare expenditures and to cut back on jobs within the public sector, we may fully expect our lower-class minorities to experience the greatest relative declines in standards of living as well as occupational opportunities. Even assuming vigorous enforcement of affirmative-action programs, there may very well be a reversal of recent trends favoring minorities and women. If so, we may also expect that white women will fare relatively better than minority members of either sex, in part because of their greater voting strength but also because of their superior educational resources and the reduced numbers of jobs requiring physical strength or stamina. Thus it would indeed be naive to assume that increasing educational equality will automatically result in corresponding relative gains for minorities in terms of either occupation or income.

Two additional kinds of questions can be noted very briefly before closing this section on empirical findings. The first concerns the relationship between the relative size of a minority and inequalities of several types. Does a large minority percentage go along with greater inequalities or lesser ones? Data comparing blacks and whites in counties and cities with varying black percentages can be used to shed light on this question. In brief, correlations between the percent of the black population and inequalities *outside* the South tend to be negligible, suggesting that any causal connections between these two types of variables are probably very indirect and, perhaps, highly complex.[29] *Within* the South, however, a number of studies have shown moderate to high correlations, with greater inequalities being associated with high percentages of blacks. One interpretation for these relationships is that a high percentage of blacks poses a political threat to whites that results in higher degrees of discrimination. Another possible interpretation involves the notion of economic competition. As the minority percentage increases, so does the degree of intergroup competition and therefore the need to discriminate.[30]

A somewhat related question is whether whites gain or lose economically as a result of discrimination against blacks. A traditional Marxist argument has been that both white and black workers lose as a result of discrimination, partly because low wages of blacks serve to depress those of whites as well, and partly because discrimination tends to divide the working classes and thereby prevent them from organizing to improve their economic situation. We have noted in the previous chapter that white laboring classes have been in the forefront of anti-minority movements. But have they been misguided in the sense that, in the long run, they have hurt their own economic position as well?

The empirical evidence is uncertain on this. Norval Glenn found that whites who live in areas having a high percentage of blacks tend to be relatively more concentrated in the white-collar occupations, suggesting that—in effect—at least a substantial portion of the white population in these areas may have benefited by relegating blacks to the least desirable occupations.[31] Albert Szymanski, taking a Marxist stance, provides another set of data to bolster the argument that white workers in states with large black-white inequalities tend, themselves, to have lowered incomes.[32] Obviously, the most impoverished areas of the country lie within the South, and it can be argued that one of the causes of these depressed conditions, for both blacks and whites, is the weakened power of labor unions. Unfortunately, however, it is very difficult to sort out the effects of a number of highly intercorrelated factors, including the nature of the area's industrial base, the quality of "human capital" (such things as the skill and educational levels of the labor force), and the level of antiminority discrimination in the locale. Thus, for the time being, we must admit that the question of white economic gains and losses has not been satisfactorily answered.

MINORITY SOCIALIZATION AND COMPETITIVE RESOURCES

The subject of differences among minority groups is a very controversial one, laden with emotionalism. If responses to discrimination differ widely across minorities, this seems to lend credence to the thesis that these minorities, themselves, are partly to blame for their condition. Such differences may then be used to justify the status quo by in effect saying: "Other minorities have made it on their own. Why can't you?" To defend a particular minority against such a charge it may then be necessary to exaggerate the handicaps under which it has been operating, while playing down those faced by other minorities that appear to have been more successful. This then tends to pit one minority against another, with each claiming that its own problems are unique and much more serious than obstacles faced by the others. This of course only makes it all the more difficult for one minority to learn from another, to say nothing of carrying on a fruitful intellectual debate designed to locate practical mechanisms for change.

Yet there are some glaring differences among minorities that seem to stem, in part, from socialization practices and the nature of the family systems that these minorities have either brought with them, in the case of migrants, or that have evolved as a result of their past histories of discrimination. Consider some miscellaneous facts:

1. The percentage of Jews who have distinguished themselves in intellectual and scientific careers is far above that of white Gentiles, and this holds true both within the United States and in virtually all countries in which Jews have had reasonably established communities.

2. The percentage of Japanese-American high-school students who complete four years of college preparatory mathematics appears to be slightly higher than that of American whites, both for males and females. But the percentage of black, Hispanic, and American Indians who take comparable math courses is considerably lower, in most instances being only about half or less that of Japanese-Americans.

3. Scores on so-called objective tests used as entrance criteria for college admissions have consistently indicated that blacks perform more poorly than whites on both verbal and quantitative reasoning. Efforts to purify these tests by deleting items that are obviously culture-bound have not succeeded in eliminating these differentials.

4. Black athletes are highly overrepresented in basketball, football, and baseball but are still very much underrepresented in upper-class sports such as golf, tennis, and swimming.

5. Overall black birth rates, illegitimacy rates, and crime rates (as measured by "official" statistics) are all considerably higher than those of whites and Asian-Americans. But the social-class *differential* in fertility rates among blacks is greater than that of whites, suggesting that middle-class blacks are, if anything, overconforming to low fertility norms.[33]

6. Insofar as adequate data are available, there are wide disparities among Asian-American minorities, with Japanese- and Chinese-Americans displaying exaggerated middle-class characteristics and Filipino-Americans tending more toward lower-class patterns.

7. In spite of initial handicaps, both Chinese- and Japanese-Americans have been much more successful in business than blacks, Indians, or Hispanics. Researcher Ivan Light attributes much of this difference to features of Chinese and Japanese cultures that supported voluntary organizations based on kinship and residence, which helped provide financial support for these business ventures.[34]

8. Studies by Rosen and others back in the 1950s showed that there are substantial differences between Jews and Italian-Americans with respect to achievement motivation, presumably stemming from different patterns of socialization within the home.[35]

When facts such as these are initially presented, there is often considerable dispute about their accuracy. Two kinds of considerations may arise. First, it may be asked whether they are real or merely artifacts of biased measurement. For instance, are the admitted differences in test scores primarily a result of imperfections in these tests, as for example a white-middle-class bias in the construction of most standardized tests? Are official crime statistics biased because of differential police arrest rates or unequal conviction rates stemming from unfair judicial sentencing practices?

When such questions are posed the result often may be a healthy discussion of just what it is that the measures are intended to tap. What is intelligence exactly? Is it even possible to design a series of tests that tap "native ability" (whatever that is), apart from the learning of specific skills? Just how are official crime data derived? What kinds of crimes are rarely if ever punished, and why are the conviction rates variable across different types of offenses? Are our crime statistics biased according to social class? If so, why? These are important questions that invariably lead to revisions in our thinking. Even if they are satisfactorily answered, however, we must still admit the possibility that there *are* some remaining differences to explain. According to our present "imperfect" measures, the murder rate among blacks appears to be eight to ten times higher than that of whites, so that even with perfect measures one would hardly expect the differences to disappear altogether. Similarly, blacks tend to do more poorly than whites on such apparently culture-free intellectual tasks as repeating a series of numbers backwards, something that very few of us practice or are ever taught to do.

The second kind of consideration is perhaps even more fundamental. Admitting that the differences exist, how do we account for them? Here is where one's intellectual biases are especially likely to enter since obviously there are multiple causes that will inevitably be very difficult to disentangle empirically. The so-called "I.Q. controversy" has generated lengthy disputes, so much so that there are only a handful of social scientists who have dared to enter the fray.[36] A similar dispute has arisen between those who have attempted to account for differences between white and black family patterns in America. The famous (or infamous) Moynihan report—which attempted to explain certain black-white differentials in terms of the "breakdown" of the black family—was almost instantaneously attacked as an effort to place the blame on the victim of discrimination, rather than on the larger white-dominated society.[37] It was also pointed out that family disorganization among black families was exaggerated by Moynihan, perhaps to make a dramatic point about the need to "save" the black family from even greater disorganization.[38]

The dispute over the black family is illustrative of many kinds of issues that are very difficult to resolve scientifically because of a lack of adequate data combined with disagreements concerning the "true causes" of the phenomena. Granted that, say, illegitimacy rates are very high among blacks, why is this the case? Some may go back to the institution of slavery, pointing out that this system was responsible for the breakdown of the African heritage, which had placed a premium on kinship as a mechanism of socialization and social control. Under slavery husbands and wives were sold to different masters, children were separated from their parents, and the household unit was deprived of its economic functions. After emancipation, the inability of black males to earn a decent living and later welfare policies that favored female-headed households over intact ones all contributed to weakening the black family. Under such conditions, the argument goes, it is indeed remarkable that black families remained viable at all.

Another sort of dispute centers around the degree of responsibility of the family in comparison with neighborhood, school, and and larger social-system variables. It can be argued that children who are brought up in ghetto "jungles" and who attend inferior schools can hardly be expected to take their mathematics lessons seriously, especially when they are also malnourished and given inferior training and counseling. Thus it is not at all fair to compare blacks and other lower-class minorities with either white ethnic groups or middle-class racial minorities such as Japanese- or Chinese-Americans. Yet many Jews were also residents of slum areas and targets of extreme hostility, not only during the early decades of the twentieth century within our own country, but also in Europe as well. How would we account, say, for differences in school performance among Jewish, Italian, Polish, Irish, or Greek immigrants?

One social-psychological line of argument is essentially that some groups stress achievement and independent thinking much more heavily than do others. As noted earlier, studies have found this to be the case among white ethnic groups, and the literature also suggests that a similar difference exists among Asian-American minorities. Jewish children, for example, are apparently encouraged at a rather early age to question what they are taught and to engage in rather abstract thought processes, a fact that may account for their remarkable success in mathematical and scientific fields. Presumably, these are skills that they bring with them into the classroom and that then interact with their formal education to produce well-above-average performance scores on examinations, as well as later academic successes.

Young black males are achieving rapid success in another very competitive field, namely professional sports, for what may be essentially the same reasons. Seeing numerous black success models on television, and being strongly motivated to develop their athletic prowess at an early age, often black youths find themselves having the clear advantage in school sports. This, in turn, motivates them to even greater efforts, as they visualize themselves as star basketball or football players with six-digit incomes and instant fame. The tragedy here, of course, is that only a very small handful will make it to the top. The rest will have invested heavily in skills that they cannot transfer to other occupations. Nevertheless, it is their socialization and work habits that are largely responsible for their high success rates. At least this seems a much more plausible explanation than one that stresses biological superiority or innate racial differences, though perhaps certain biologically relevant factors such as average height and build cannot be ruled out as contributing causes.

One problem with all of these explanations is that there is a "mix" of factors responsible for racial and ethnic differences in outcome variables. Do we decide which variables are most important by listening to those who shout the loudest, by accepting whatever set of beliefs happens to be the fad of the day, or that satisfy our own vested interests? In instances where there are multiple causes involved, as well as reasonably high intercorrelations among some of the explanatory variables, how can we proceed in a more rational fashion? Although the subject is complex, and certainly not confined to this single topic, it is important to try to attach quantitative weights to the several factors involved as illustrated by the status-attainment models discussed earlier. At this point we simply do not have adequate enough data or theories to provide definitive information about these issues.

Obviously, a detailed consideration of differences among minorities would require substantially more discussion of specific groups—and the situations they each face—than is possible in this brief overview. The purpose in bringing up the subject in this rather superficial fashion, however, is to call the reader's attention to a series of issues that are often either left undiscussed or are the subject of considerable ideological debate, rather than scientific appraisal. It is also an area that requires the kind of in-depth knowledge of each specific minority that is often best obtained by first-hand experience in that minority's subculture.

NOTES

1. See Gerhard Lenski, "Marxist Experiments in Destratification: An Appraisal," *Social Forces,* 57 (1978), pp. 364–83. *Deciles* are positions in a frequency distribution that divide this distribution into ten equal-sized portions.

2. For general discussions of inequality see Peter M. Blau, *Inequality and Heterogeneity: A Primitive Theory of Social Structure* (New York: Free Press, 1977); Gerhard Lenski, *Power and Privilege,* (New York: McGraw-Hill, 1966); and Christopher Jencks, et al., *Inequality: A Reassessment of the Effect of Family and Schooling in America* (New York: Basic Books, 1972).

3. The standard deviation, defined statistically as the square root of the variance (about a mean), has a very simple property in the case of approximately normally distributed variables. If one knows how many standard deviations one is from the mean, one can tell approximately how many cases will be above or below this figure. *Quartiles* divide a frequency distribution into four equal-sized parts.

4. See Kingsley Davis and Wilbert E. Moore, "Some Principles of Stratification," *American Sociological Review,* 10 (1945), pp. 242–49.

5. Lenski, *Power and Privilege,* chaps. 1-3.

6. See Otis Dudley Duncan, "A Socioeconomic Index for All Occupations," in Albert J. Reiss, et al., (eds.), *Occupations and Social Status* (New York: Free Press, 1961), pp. 109-38; see also, Donald J. Treiman, *Occupational Prestige in Comparative Perspective* (New York: Academic Press, 1977).

7. For an elementary discussion of this and other issues relating to causal diagrams see H. M. Blalock, *Causal Inferences in Nonexperimental Research* (Chapel Hill: University of North Carolina Press, 1964), chaps. 1-3.

8. Whenever an arrow is omitted, this implies that since there is no direct link between the two variables, if one controls simultaneously for all antecedent causes and intervening variables, the association between these two variables should disappear. This testable prediction may then be assessed in terms of one's data.

9. See Peter M. Blau and Otis Dudley Duncan, *The American Occupational Structure* (New York: Wiley, 1967), chaps. 5 and 6.

10. The literature on path coefficients is now becoming extensive, and the basic ideas are presented in many elementary statistics texts. The essential points to understand are that each coefficient (see Figure 3) represents a measure of the *direct* effects of one variable on another and that the coefficients have been made comparable across different variables that may be measured in terms of very different units (such as dollars versus years). However, these standardized measures are *noncomparable* across different populations, which may differ with respect to their standard deviations. If, say, we wish to compare blacks and whites with respect to increments in annual incomes associated with each increment in years of schooling (say, $800 for blacks and $1200 for whites), then such standardized measures should *not* be used. In this latter instance we may use, instead, what are called (ordinary) regression coefficients that measure the amount of change in one variable for a unit change in another, as expressed in terms of whatever units of measurement have been selected.

11. Otis Dudley Duncan, David L. Featherman, and Beverly Duncan, *Socioeconomic Background and Achievement* (New York: Seminar Press, 1972), p. 103.

12. It is conventional to insert ordinary correlation coefficients (instead of path coefficients) alongside such curved arrows to indicate the magnitudes of the unexplained associations among these variables.

13. If one squares the numerical coefficients associated with these side arrows one obtains the proportion of the variance in the dependent variable that is *unexplained* by all of the remaining variables that affect it. Thus a value of .7 attached to such an arrow means that 49 percent of the variance remains to be explained.

14. See David L. Featherman and Robert M. Hauser, *Opportunity and Change* (New York: Academic Press, 1978), chaps. 2 and 3.

15. See: James N. Porter, "Race, Socialization and Mobility in Educational and Early Occupational Attainment," *American Sociological Review,* 39 (1974), pp. 303-16; Alan C. Kerckhoff and K. T. Campbell, "Race and Social Status Differences

in the Explanation of Educational Ambition," *Social Forces,* 55 (1977), pp. 701–14; and Gail E. Thomas, "The Influence of Ascription, Achievement and Educational Expectations on Black-White Postsecondary Enrollment," *Sociological Quarterly,* 20 (1979), pp. 209–222.

16. See especially Morris Rosenberg and R. A. Simmons, *Black and White Self-Esteem: The Urban School Child* (Washington, D.C.: American Sociological Association, 1972); and Edgar G. Epps, "The Impact of School Desegregation on Aspirations, Self-Concepts and Other Aspects of Personality," *Law and Contemporary Problems,* 39 (1975), pp. 300–13.

17. Featherman and Hauser, *Opportunity and Change,* chap. 8.

18. Jencks, et al., *Inequality,* chap. 9.

19. See Ross M. Stolzenberg, "Black/White Differences in Occupation, Education, and Wages," *American Journal of Sociology,* 81 (1975), pp. 299–323; see also, Erik Olin Wright and Luca Perrone, "Marxist Class Categories and Income Inequality," *American Sociological Review,* 42 (1977), pp. 32–55.

20. Wright and Perrone, "Marxist Class Categories and Income Inequality." See also Erik Olin Wright, "Race, Class, and Income Inequality," *American Journal of Sociology,* 83 (1978), pp. 1368–97; and Joe L. Spaeth, "Vertical Differentiation Among Occupations," *American Sociological Review,* 44 (1979), pp. 746–62.

21. Duncan, et al., (*Socioeconomic Background and Achievement,* p. 56) report that the slope of the relationship between fathers' and sons' occupations is less steep in the case of blacks than in the case of whites. Similarly, Featherman and Hauser (*Opportunity and Change*) report weaker associations between parental characteristics and those of the son in the case of blacks, though they also suggest that mobility patterns among *younger* blacks are apparently becoming more predictable than those for older generations of blacks. This may well be due to expanding opportunities for blacks. See their chap. 6.

22. For a detailed review of these trends see Reynolds Farley, "Trends in Racial Inequalities: Have the Gains in the 1960s Disappeared in the 1970s?" *American Sociological Review,* 42 (1977), pp. 189–207.

23. Over and above the problem of measuring "ability," we have the additional one of trying to specify exactly what learning-related characteristics are of interest, say, to employers. Is it specialized knowledge, ability to think abstractly, motivation to work hard, intellectual flexibility, or what?

24. Although certainly not original with them, this thesis is given empirical support in the quantitative study by Featherman and Hauser, *Opportunity and Change.*

25. See Farley, "Trends in Racial Inequalities."

26. See note 21.

27. The percentage of single-parent households among blacks was 47.8 percent in 1978, as compared with 23 percent in 1960. Of these, practically all involved female rather than male parents (in 1978, 45 percent compared to 2.7 percent). Although the percentage of single-parent families among whites also doubled during this period (from 7 percent to 15 percent), the much lower starting point among whites means that the *gap* between black and white percentages has increased dramatically during the past two decades. See table 3, p. 9, of the Current Population Reports, Special Studies, Series P-23, Number 84, U.S. Department of Commerce, Bureau of the Census, 1979.

28. See Farley, "Trends in Racial Inequalities."

29. For a review of this literature see Jerry Wilcox and Wade Clark Roof, "Percent Black and Black-White Status Inequality: Southern Versus Nonsouthern Patterns," *Social Science Quarterly,* 59 (1978), pp. 421–34.

30. For a theoretical statement of this thesis see H. M. Blalock, *Toward a Theory of Minority-Group Relations,* chap. 5.

31. See Norval Glenn, "Occupational Benefits to Whites from the Subordination of Negroes," *American Sociological Review,* 28 (1963), pp. 443–48; and Norval Glenn, "White Gains from Negro Subordination," *Social Problems,* 14 (1966), pp. 159–78.

32. See Albert Szymanski, "Racial Discrimination and White Gain," *American Sociological Review,* 41 (1976), 403–14. See also Michael Reich, "The Economics of

Racism," in D. M. Gordon (ed.). *Problems in Political Economy: An Urban Perspective* (Lexington, Mass.: Heath, 1971), pp. 107-13.

33. See Samuel H. Preston, "Differential Fertility, Unwanted Fertility, and Racial Trends in Occupational Achievement," *American Sociological Review,* 39 (1974), pp. 492-506.

34. Ivan H. Light, *Ethnic Enterprise in America* (Berkeley: University of California Press, 1972).

35. See especially Bernard C. Rosen, "Race, Ethnicity, and the Achievement Syndrome," *American Sociological Review,* 24 (1959), pp. 47-60.

36. This debate became renewed with the publication of the controversial article by Arthur R. Jensen, "How Much Can We Boost IQ and Scholastic Achievement?" *Harvard Educational Review,* 39 (1969), pp. 1-123. For a critical review of this literature, written from a black perspective, see Howard Taylor, *The I.Q. Game* (New Brunswick: Rutgers University Press, 1980).

37. See Daniel P. Moynihan, *The Negro Family: The Case for National Action* (Washington, D.C.: U.S. Department of Labor, 1965). See also Lee Rainwater and William L. Yancey, *The Moynihan Report and the Politics of Controversy* (Cambridge, Mass.: M.I.T. Press, 1967).

38. See Andrew Billingsley, *Black Families in White America* (Englewood Cliffs, N.J.: Prentice-Hall, 1968. The Moynihan Report is discussed in the Appendix of Billingsley's book.

CHAPTER 6
SEGREGATION
AND INTERGROUP
INTERACTIONS

The saying "Birds of a feather flock together" is an old observation which recognizes the fact that similar individuals have a tendency to prefer each other's company, for any number of reasons. In fact, the idea that segregation is a "natural" phenomenon is often used as a justification for many types of regulations that directly or indirectly *impose* this separation on persons identified as members of different groups. And it is also used to justify opposing laws or administrative practices that are intended to break down these same patterns of segregation. Thus in many cities where blacks have been prevented by real-estate and banking policies from moving out of segregated ghetto areas, there is also strong opposition to mandatory busing, designed to bring school children of different races into contact who happen to live in different parts of the city.

There are basically two kinds of variables with which we will be concerned in this chapter. The first concerns territoriality and refers to *spatial* separation. This is the notion of "segregation," and as we shall see later in the chapter it is measured in terms of the numbers of persons (or families) living in close proximity to each other. The second refers to the extensiveness of interaction and could be measured in terms of the proportion of cross-group *contacts* that take place. Where this proportion of cross-group contacts approximates what we would expect by chance under complete mixing, we shall refer to this situation as being one of a high degree of "integration."

Segregation, then, refers to spatial separation, whereas *integration* refers to interaction patterns, and thus the two concepts are not polar opposites. It is possible, though somewhat rare, to have two groups who are residentially almost totally segregated from one another and yet have a high degree of interaction. More common is to find two groups living close to one another and yet for the interactions between them to be constrained or at least highly regulated. We shall have occasion to discuss this latter situation in more detail, for it often occurs when two groups must live close to each other and also engage in specified types of contacts, as for example those necessary in a market economy. This does not necessarily mean, however, that they will interact as social equals or that they will regard each other as anything other than complete strangers.

Usually, of course, a high degree of spatial segregation implies very little contact between two groups. There are many reasons why patterns of segregation tend to be maintained, even where on the surface they are highly disadvantageous to one or both groups. We shall examine some of these reasons later in the chapter. Often members of a dominant group will claim that minority segregation is "voluntary" and actually preferred, and to some extent this will always be the case. One might note a certain degree of hypocrisy in such an assertion, however, if the "preference" for segregation results from minority mistreatment or fear of injury, from a concern that one will be rebuffed, or from a general uncomfortableness in the presence of those who continually look down upon members of one's own group. Why, for example, should a black or Chicano family want to live in a white neighborhood if they expect their children to be rejected or subjected to threats? To refer to self-imposed segregation under such circumstances as "voluntary" is to put the cart before the horse.

Before turning our attention to matters that are directly relevant to American minorities, it is important to stress that there are numerous racial and ethnic groups worldwide who make strong territorial claims stemming from historical patterns, memories of which are transmitted and made very conspicuous to each new generation. Often, such groups have become subordinate minorities as a result of conquest, and in many instances have either been driven from land they previously inhabited or have been awarded only a fraction of this original territory. Usually these ethnic groups retain important cultural features such as a distinct language or dialect, dress, religious practices, and kinship patterns that clearly mark them off from the surrounding majority. Language, especially, becomes a crucial distinguishing characteristic, since it not only has symbolic importance but is also obviously a necessary feature of one's economic, religious, and social institutions.

Today, as well as throughout earlier historical epochs, we see many instances in which these territorial claims of ethnic groups are closely linked with separatist movements or clamors for greater autonomy. Basques in northern Spain, Croatians in Yugoslavia, Kurds in Iran, Iraq, and Turkey, and of course Palestinians located in Lebanon, Jordan, and Israel are constantly making headlines as a result of terrorist activities, but these are merely the extreme instances. The Ukrainian and Georgian minorities within the Soviet Union also periodically come to our attention, and we must infer that they are continually making more "trouble" for the Soviet government than the latter will freely admit. Basically, what most of these minorities want—if they cannot gain true independence—is to be left alone to govern themselves internally and to continue traditional ways.

One of the major tragedies resulting from past human migrations and conflicts is the fact that claim over much of the world's desirable land is often disputed by several groups simultaneously, and each can point to a specific historical period in its glorious past during which that territory was, in fact, occupied by its own ancestors. This is, of course, one of the core issues in the Arab-Israeli dispute over Jerusalem, a fact that is made all the more complicated by religious extremists on both sides who are able to claim holy scriptures in support of their own rigid positions. Such disputes are common almost everywhere, resulting from long histories of migrations and conquests. As noted earlier, the manner in which the continent of Africa was carved up among European powers has left us with a number of tiny nations, the boundaries of which seldom correspond to ethnic or tribal claims. Throughout the world, then, there are a bewildering number of internal minorities, each with its own territorial claims and ideological supports for the legitimacy of these claims.

The situation in the United States is, however, quite different, because our largest minority, blacks, was not displaced from territory it occupied on this continent. Instead blacks were forced immigrants who for economic reasons were settled primarily within the Southern portions of the country. For this reason, although geographically concentrated in that region until very recently, few blacks have ever claimed that the South was their territorial domain. Instead, they have steadily migrated outward, with little sentimental attachment to that area. Though presently located primarily within the central cities of our largest metropolitan areas, there is likewise no general claim that these locations should belong to blacks, or that they are their rightful territories. A similar picture holds true for Puerto Rican migrants to the U.S. mainland and for all of the Asian-American minorities.

The situation for Chicanos is a mixed one, since many members of this minority can trace their ancestry to portions of today's United States that were given up by Mexico as a result of conquest. Other Chicanos have migrated to this country since that time. Our "purest" case of a minority with distinct territorial claims is that of the American Indians, who, however, constitute a very small fraction of the American population. A detailed examination of this minority—which cannot be attempted in this work—would no doubt uncover a number of similarities between its situation and those of many other "displaced" minorities in Eastern Europe, Africa, Latin America, and Asia. We suspect—though evidence is not systematically available—that this type of minority is far more likely to be separatist in orientation than is the minority whose members have, for the most part, rather recently entered an area through migration, even where this migration was forced. The current separatist movement among French Canadians is a case in point, as are those of Basques, Kurds, and Croatians.[1]

RESIDENTIAL SEGREGATION IN
AMERICAN CITIES

Where we live partly determines many things, including the places where we shop, recreate, dine, send our children to school, and even where some of us work. It also determines whom we see most often as neighbors, as well as the friendship cliques we join. Therefore residential segregation constitutes an important mechanism affecting many other kinds of segregation. In particular, the whole question of busing to achieve racial balance is intimately bound to that of residential segregation. If blacks and other minorities were evenly distributed throughout all residential neighborhoods there would obviously be no need to bus children.

It is therefore crucial to determine just how much residential segregation exists and whether the degree of such segregation is increasing or decreasing. It is also important to know more about the factors that influence the degree of segregation. Are all minorities equally segregated from the predominant white Protestant population? If not, what accounts for the differences? What have been the trends throughout the past five or six decades, and what would we predict if these trends were to continue unabated?

Unfortunately, we do not always have the necessary information to answer every one of these questions, but there is, in fact, a substantial body of literature on the subject, though the available data for the most part are applicable only to the largest cities of the United States and are not quite comparable from one decade to the next. This is often the case with respect to data that social scientists are unable to collect for themselves, since they are, in effect, at the mercy of the Census Bureau or other federal agencies. For example, it would be highly desirable to have information about the residential patterns of different religious groups, especially Jewish-Gentile residential locations. We would also like to have separate data on individual Hispanic and Asian-American groups, as well as data for rural areas and smaller urban communities. But such data are simply not available.

The first thing to note about the concept of segregation is that it refers to a structural property of a group—in this case the population of a city—and not to individual persons. That is, although we might speak crudely about individuals being segregated from each other within a city, our *measure* of the degree of segregation (in terms of a "segregation score") would have to be attached to the city (or other macro-unit), rather than to the person. Thus we may obtain a segregation score of 96 for Dallas and compare it with one of 77 for New York, but it would make no sense to develop a segregation score for John Smith, apart from saying that he lives within a highly segregated district of a given city.

The measure that is commonly used to indicate the degree of residential segregation is basically a refinement of a very simple, commonsense idea.[2] It first requres that we subdivide a city (or some other territory) into subunits of a specified nature. The simplest and most convenient such unit, when the data are available, is the city block, defined by the Census as being the territory enclosed by intersecting streets. Having chopped up our imaginary city into subunits, and supposing as an example that our minority constitutes 20 percent of the city's population, then we may define zero segregation as that situation in which there is a completely uniform percentage of the minority, here 20 percent, within *all* of the subunits. In contrast, there will be complete segregation (scored as 100) whenever every block contains either all whites or all blacks—that is, whenever every white person in the city lives within an all-white block and every black within an all-black block.

Needless to say, there will be many blocks that contain intermediate percentages of blacks and whites, and we will thus need a measure of segregation that ranges between 0 and 100, with the intermediate values (say, 60) being clearly interpretable. One rather simple way of constructing such an interpretable measure is to ask what percentage of the blacks (or whites) would need to be moved from their actual locations in order to obtain a completely uniform distribution (or zero segregation). If, for example, 80 percent of the blacks would need to be moved into predominantly white areas, this would constitute a higher degree of segregation than if only 40 percent would need to be moved. The Index of Dissimilarity (ID) is a very general type of measure that can be applied to segregation and, in fact, has exactly this kind of interpretation.

The most important finding using the ID measure is one that will come as no surprise to American readers. Studies using block data have found that blacks and whites are extremely segregated from each other in practically *all* American cities regardless of region, size of city (above 100,000), relative size of the black community, or even the relative economic position of blacks and whites. Taeuber and Taeuber, for example, found that for 207 cities in 1960 the median ID score was approximately 87.8, indicating that for the "typical" American city fully 88 percent of the black population would have to be moved to predominantly white blocks in order to achieve a uniform distribution.[3] The mean ID score for Southern cities was 90.0 as compared with the national mean (rather than the median) of 86.2. The mean scores for the Northeast, North Central, and West were, respectively, 79.2, 87.7, and 79.3.[4] In 1970, using a slightly different regional classification, Taeuber and his associates obtained mean segregation scores as follows: South 91.4; North 81.4; Border States 87.3, and West 81.1.[5] Thus there was no evidence of a decline in residential segregation during the decade of the 1960s.

Clearly, these uniformly high segregation levels for blacks suggest that residential segregation is not caused by economic differentials alone, an inference that is further supported by findings that adjustments for economic differences between the races account for only a small portion of this extensive segregation. Put differently, even if whites and blacks were suddenly to find their economic positions identical, a very substantial amount of residential segregation would be expected to persist. This is in contrast to trends found in the case of white ethnic minorities for which the more moderate levels of segregation have been decreasing over the past half-century. Though truly adequate information is unavailable, we presume that residential segregation of Chicanos and Puerto Ricans falls intermediate between that of blacks and of white ethnic groups. Figures for specific Asian-American minorities are also lacking, but apparently Chinese-Americans remain relatively more segregated than Japanese-Americans, in spite of their earlier arrival in America.

What accounts for such extremely high levels of racial segregation in American cities, as well as elsewhere around the world? Clearly, someone must be benefiting from these patterns. In the remainder of this chapter we shall briefly examine some of the "rewards" or segregation gains for diverse parties.

"VOLUNTARY" SEGREGATION

For groups that have become minorities as a result of conquest, segregation is a means of self-preservation and a mechanism for maintaining a previously successful way of life. It also facilitates the socialization of younger generations and inhibits them from migrating to urban areas where their minority identification would become diluted. Also, a similar pattern of voluntary segregation is found among small religious sects, for although they may not be especially subjected to discrimination or persecution, they see segregation as virtually the only way of maintaining their cultural heritage in the face of an environment that is hostile or subversive to its survival.

Many such minorities do not come to our attention as "problem" minorities unless, of course, they make trouble for members of the dominant group. Basques in France, for example, present nothing like the problems that this same minority do in Spain, probably because the territory they occupy in the French Pyrenees is only of marginal importance to the French economy, whereas the land occupied by the Spanish Basques is of much greater economic significance to that nation. Thus if a minority has managed to locate itself on land of no significance to the dominant group, its autonomy may be assured for a prolonged period of time. Most American Indian tribes have not been this fortunate, but a few have.

Immigrant minorities face a very different problem, especially if the migration takes place over a prolonged period of time. Here the advantages of segregation accrue primarily to individual migrants and nuclear families, who require a period of adjustment and assistance prior to assimilating into the predominant culture. In the United States we witnessed a long sequence of white European immigration, with one ethnic group after another entering at the very bottom of the occupational ladder, initially ill-equipped to cope with the English language and local customs, and needing considerable aid in locating housing, jobs, welfare assistance, and general psychic support. Many of these immigrants were preceded by relatives or friends from the same village. It is no wonder, then, that they chose to locate in the same few Eastern ports of entry and to congregate in the same neighborhoods where they could enjoy the security provided by old friends and others who could speak their language, as well as by familiar religious and social institutions patterned along the lines of those from the old country.

Insofar as segregation of these immigrant groups was based entirely on these adjustment needs, we would expect the degree of residential segregation of a given minority to be reduced with each successive generation. This has in fact been the case, up to a point, with most of our white ethnic minorities. Yet recent studies of residential segregation among these groups have shown that the degree of segregation is still somewhat higher than one would expect on the basis of occupation and income alone.[6] That is, there is still a tendency for these groups to hold together in spite of a more general movement toward dispersal, and we would infer from this fact either that their members still face barriers to geographic mobility similar to those faced by racial minorities or that this remaining residential segregation is by preference. Segregation by preference, of course, would be partially attributable to simple inertia—such things as the ownership of valuable properties or businesses or a reluctance to move from the area of one's childhood. But, presumably, a certain proportion of these persons remain partly segregated because of the benefits of living in close proximity to those having similar ethnic backgrounds or to ethnic churches or other institutions.

Some individual minority members will profit directly from segregation and therefore may have a vested interest in its perpetuation, though they may disguise this interest in terms of what they claim to be the minority's own welfare. For example, the owners or managers of small businesses, religious leaders who depend upon a geographic concentration for large attendance at church services, and politicians who would not otherwise be elected to office, all stand to gain through the perpetuation of segregated communities. Moreover, institutions as well as neighborhoods can be segregated in this way. Black colleges in the South contain some black faculty who would find it difficult to compete in the open market and who therefore resist the notion that black students should attend predominantly white colleges and universities. Since there will always be plausible arguments in favor of maintaining such segregated institutions until some unspecified time in the future, we can expect that a minority that has been able to develop such institutions over an extensive period of time will be ambivalent about giving them up. Furthermore, resistance to integration can be expected to come from certain elite groups within the minority itself.

Having said this we must remember, however, that much segregation is *not* voluntary. Historical and contemporary examples of *involuntary* segregation abound: Blacks have been prevented from moving out of racial ghettos by various devices. During certain historical periods Jews have been confined to ghetto areas and even literally imprisoned within them. (Perhaps the most infamous example in recent history of enforced segregation was the Warsaw ghetto, which became a staging place for mass genocide of Jews during the later years of Hitler's occupation.) On other occasions segregation has been used as a temporary device, as for example the "interning" of Japanese-Americans during World War II. And, although not presently enforced by law, residential segregation of blacks and Chicanos is reinforced by a number of mechanisms that clearly have the strong support of many if not most white Americans. We must look, then, at some of the reasons why dominant groups throughout the world have often strongly encouraged, if not actually required, spatial segregation and, in addition, at how unavoidable intergroup contact is regulated, contact which could not actually be prevented without incurring unusual costs.

WHAT DOMINANT GROUPS GAIN FROM SEGREGATION

A certain amount of segregation will *indirectly* result from economic discrimination. Since, for example, black-family incomes are only about 60 percent of those of whites, obviously many blacks cannot afford expensive housing in predominantly white suburbia, regardless of whether or not there is any effort to exclude them from these neighborhoods. Most persons will tend to live near their place of work, so that if minorities are not hired in certain industries, or if they constitute only a tiny fraction of the membership of a given profession, this may also tend to exclude them from a number of residential areas.

However, in addition to indirect causes of residential segregation, there are a number of more *direct causes* as well. Often minorities find themselves unwanted in certain residential areas, even where their incomes or occupations would permit their entry. They may, in some instances, even be forbidden by law to live in certain sections of a city. More commonly they are kept out by a number of more informal but nevertheless highly effective devices. These forms of segregation provide dominant groups with several specific advantages.

Segregation often makes it easier for dominant groups to maintain this dominance, or at least to divert resources and services from the minority to its own members. It has already been noted that, as industries continue to decentralize by moving to suburban locations, this provides an advantage to those who live in these suburbs. Those who live in ghetto areas, for example, are much less likely to hear about new job openings and are also handicapped by greater travel costs.

Segregated neighborhoods permit governmental and private agencies to provide services of unequal quality to different racial or ethnic groups, and this includes educational and health institutions as well. Especially in metropolitan areas where the central city is primarily minority occupied while the politically autonomous suburbs are virtually all white, there is usually a gross inequality in tax rates coupled with one-sided use of city and suburban facilities. Suburban residents often use city libraries, mass transit, parks, zoos, and other amenities that are paid for primarily out of city-based rather than suburban-based funding.

Obviously, this both works to the disadvantage of minorities and others who live within city limits and serves as an incentive to those who can do so to join the suburban movement. Thus there is a major economic vested interest in residential segregation as a means of diverting services from minorities and assuring dominant-group members that their own services can be maintained at a relatively lower cost.

These economic advantages of segregation that accrue to general members of the dominant group are reinforced by other advantages which go primarily to certain "gatekeepers" of residential segregation, namely, realtors and lending institutions. Until rather recently these two "gatekeepers" have been able to maintain a very tight control over the movements of blacks through a number of devices. One of the earlier mechanisms, which was also used against Jews and many other minority groups, was the so-called "restrictive covenant" that was usually imposed on new buyers. This was basically an agreement prohibiting the buyer from selling to specified categories of persons.

When these covenants were declared unenforceable by the Supreme Court in 1948 they were typically replaced by "gentlemen's agreements" that were intended to have the same effect. Minority members were simply not shown homes in white or all-Gentile neighborhoods, and if one or two slipped through the realtor's sieve few sellers were willing to risk the disapproval of their friends and neighbors. Banks contributed to segregation by refusing mortgages to minority members unless they were purchasing homes in "appropriate" areas, namely, those in which their own groups constituted the overwhelming majority or which were believed to be in transition to minority areas.

These practices of realtors and lending institutions were buttressed by strongly held popular beliefs that property values would be adversely affected if minority members were to enter white-Gentile neighborhoods, even in small numbers. Although a series of scientific studies done in the 1950s provided evidence to discredit this myth, they had virtually no impact on these popular beliefs, which are still subscribed to today.[7] The real fear, of course, was not so much that property values would decline as that neighborhood racial composition would be drastically altered. In many neighborhoods bordering on black ghettos this fear was, in fact, substantiated, because, since expanding minorities were bottled up in overcrowded areas, they were able to move out only selectively in a few directions at a time. Once a neighborhood was "busted" and a few black families had moved in, there was then a steady increase in the minority percentage until the area concerned had been "taken over."

Realtors and lending institutions also profited by this "blockbusting" process, often deliberately encouraging black migration into selected areas while stimulating panic selling among white homeowners. For those owners who sold to middlemen, practically always at below-market prices, there did appear to be a loss in property values. The minority *buyers* would then be asked to pay a premium price, however, with the middleman pocketing the difference. This practice served to perpetuate the illusion among these sellers that property *values* were being affected. Another practice that of "redlining," has also recently come under attack. This is the practice among lending institutions of, in effect, drawing boundaries around certain sections of a city and refusing to make loans in these areas unless they are to the right persons.

Both blockbusting and redlining are now coming under closer scrutiny, as are the discriminatory practices of real-estate agents who fail to show available homes to minority customers. We may anticipate, however, that more subtle devices will continue to operate, though perhaps with less effectiveness than in the recent past. For one thing, the threat of legal action is an important mechanism for inhibiting the most blatant of these discriminatory practices, and a greater white acceptance of blacks and other minorities seems to have removed some of the normative underpinnings for these practices.

On the level of the individual dominant-group member, the motivation or utility for segregation derives from a number of factors in addition to the strictly economic ones. Once a minority has been socially defined as having low status and as having a number of undesirable characteristics, any dominant-group member who associates with that minority may expect to lose status as a result of this contact.[8] The expected status loss will vary with the nature of the contact. Certain very casual or "unavoidable" contacts will not be sanctioned. But highly intimate ones and those that normally imply a near-equality among contact partners will tend to be avoided because of this expected status loss. For example, one ordinarily invites to dinner and recreates with those persons who are approximately one's social peers, and one is judged socially by the company one keeps, so to speak.

Many social clubs and friendship cliques are informally ranked in much the same way. Belonging to an "elite" community club is an important device for assuring status, and this mechanism carries over to relationships with minority members. After all, an "exclusive" club is one that, by definition, excludes people. An occasional exception may be admitted, especially if the minority person is a celebrity. Thus a black campus athlete may be eagerly sought out as a fraternity pledge, just as a minority political leader or prominent clergyman may also be included as a token member of one's social circle. But the acceptance of more ordinary minority members would represent an admission that one's social circle is several notches lower in status than that of others that maintain the exclusion. A similar pattern holds for much more informal, flexible, and open-ended friendship cliques, as well as visitation relationships among neighbors.

The "ultimate" degree of intimate contact is marriage. Ethnic and racial groups who wish to maintain their boundaries as distinct groups must find ways of keeping intermarriage rates at an extremely low level. This is one of the major themes of the work *Ethnic Groups and Boundaries* in which a group of anthropologically oriented social scientists discuss a number of boundary-maintaining mechanisms.[9] It was also a major thesis of Gunnar Myrdal in his work *An American Dilemma*.[10] Myrdal argued that at the very top of the hierarchy of white American taboos regarding contacts with blacks was the bar against intermarriage.

He claimed that other concerns about contact are intimately linked to this fear of intermarriage. The basic idea had also been researched much earlier by Emory S. Bogardus who, in 1928, developed a social-distance scale through which resistances to various forms of contact with minorities were compared.[11]

The basic idea behind both the social-distance scale and Myrdal's argument is that members of any given group—particularly a dominant one—will be most resistant to admitting a member of another group into their own immediate families through intermarriage. They will be somewhat less resistant to potentially threatening "social" contacts, as for example inviting a minority member as an overnight guest or admitting one into a close friendship circle. Somewhat less important would be admitting a minority family into one's neighborhood or into one's club or church group, and so on.

A whole series of scientific studies using the social-distance scale have confirmed that there is a uniform hierarchy of preferences regarding the degree of intimacy permitted different minority groups.[12] Minorities in the United States can be ranked in a descending hierarchy according to the average degree of intimacy permitted. Not surprisingly, this hierarchy "list" of minorities remains almost constant across all raters, regardless of their own racial or ethnic group. The exception is that each minority rates itself at or near the top in terms of preferred contacts, but it tends to rate all of the *other* minorities in exactly the same order, as do the dominant white-Gentiles. Blacks are at or near the very bottom of each group's hierarchy, with the obvious exception that blacks rate other blacks at the top. It has also been found that persons who tend to give lower ratings to all ethnic groups other than their own will even reject *fictitious* groups (such as "Wallonians"), with whom they could not possibly have had previous contacts!

This very heavy emphasis on preventing intermarriage and thus a high degree of intimacy undoubtedly is still a major reason for the extreme resistance that many white parents have toward interracial and even interethnic contacts within the school setting. Prior to the Supreme Court's landmark desegregation decision, *Brown* v. *Board of Education* (1954), which outlawed segregation in public schools, a series of lesser decisions had led Southern officials to believe that desegregation could be avoided, provided that black and white schools were equalized with respect to such things as teacher salaries, building and library facilities, and teacher-pupil ratios. This produced an almost desperate effort within most Southern communities to equalize these facilities—often at considerable financial cost—so as to preserve a totally segregated system.

This economically "nonrational" response clearly seems due to a very strong desire, if not an outright obsession, to preserve segregation. Today, Northern resistance to mandatory busing to achieve racial balance, though sometimes rationalized in economic terms, also appears to be motivated by the same goal. Although there are other factors involved in this Northern resistance—including a concern that the quality of the children's education will suffer and that interracial tensions will be high—there undoubtedly are a very large number of white parents who simply do not want their children to associate with black children, as well as a lesser proportion of black parents who also prefer a segregated system. Thus the widespread insistence on reinstating "neighborhood schools" appears to be not a concern for convenience and tradition but a smokescreen to block interracial contact.

Segregation also provides important psychic protections for members of both the dominant and minority groups. Almost by definition we all like to avoid unpleasant, potentially embarrassing, or ambiguous contact situations. For this reason we prefer contacts with partners whose behaviors can be predicted reasonably accurately and whose interests and perspectives are most compatible with our own. Thus liberals tend to avoid contacts with conservatives, religious fundamentalists with agnostics, beer drinkers with teetotalers, and academics with antiintellectuals. Especially where two groups are already highly segregated and culturally very distinct it will generally be uncomfortable to try to bridge the gap, and most individuals will simply not try to do so.

Where misunderstandings are likely to arise and where economic interests are divergent or tension levels high, most actors on both sides will anticipate that contacts will produce a high degree of hostility, and even possible injury. Because the behavior of the other party is difficult to predict, there is likely to be a high degree of anticipated ambiguity and embarrassment involved. Fear of this tends to produce avoidance behavior on the part of typical members of both groups. Why engage in such contacts when there are plenty of alternative partners available?

Finally, segregation serves as a guilt reduction mechanism for many members of a dominant group. "Out of sight, out of mind" is the popular saying relevant to this phenomenon. If whites cannot see the living conditions being faced by a minority, and if their children do not go to the same schools, it then becomes rather easy to believe that opportunities available to the minority are in fact equal to those of the dominant group. American Indians who are isolated in impoverished reservations may remain totally unnoticed by the larger white population until there is some "disturbance" that gives the minority visibility. Gunnar Myrdal used the phrase "convenient ignorance" to characterize the predominant orientation of Northern whites concerning the condition of blacks some thirty-five years ago.[13] This same phrase seems equally appropriate today.

Those minorities who have adopted a separatist orientation often fail to give due consideration to this important dominant-group guilt-reduction mechanism. If a minority really wants to go it alone, it may be argued, then they should be permitted to do so—without any help. The fact that the minority may have been relegated to extremely poor land, or that its resources may have been previously taken away, may also be conveniently ignored. Unless a substantial number of dominant-group members inadvertently pass through the minority territory, they will have no way of verifying the claims of the minority. And if they almost never have face-to-face intimate contacts with minority members they will rarely be motivated to do so, even if they occasionally catch a glimpse of that minority in their midst. Social programs aimed at improving the minority's position will never gain dominant-group support, or they will, at best, be given extremely low priority.

THE REGULATION OF INTERGROUP CONTACTS

Suppose members of a dominant group wish to maintain their favored position but realize that contacts with a minority cannot be avoided for practical reasons. For instance, in many small Southern communities there are numerous blacks and whites who interact daily, either on the job or at least routinely during the course of everyday activities. In such communities, where people are rather intimately acquainted with each other's affairs, it would be totally impractical to keep the two groups apart. Similarly, in India there are numerous castes and subcastes, with each local village containing at least several distinct groupings that are hierarchically arranged in terms of prestige.

Under such circumstances we commonly find that contacts between members of these different groups will be *regulated* by custom and, on some occasions, by actual laws that forbid specified interactions to take place. The notion of caste "pollution" is also common under these circumstances. For instance, in India there are an extensive series of taboos focused on the taking of food and drink, with members of higher castes becoming "polluted" if they accept, say, water from a member of a lower caste.

A similar set of practices and beliefs existed until very recently in many Southern communities, particularly in the Deep South.[14] Contact between blacks and whites was regulated, first of all, by many kinds of deference behaviors that served to emphasize the status gap between the two groups. Black men were called "boy" regardless of their age or were sometimes given ridiculously exaggerated titles such as "Professor" or "Captain." Black women would be referred to by their first names, or by such titles as "Auntie" or "Mammy." Whites, in contrast, had to be called "Mister" or "Ma'am" or "Missus," again regardless of age, occupation, or local reputation. Blacks were expected to use highly exaggerated gestures of subservience, such as the bowed-head, hat-in-hand, foot-scuffling behavior epitomized in the minstrel shows of the early 1900s. They were expected to enter white homes only by the back door and to initiate conversations either only when necessary or in such a fashion that their low status was clearly emphasized. Blacks were also expected to smile and joke and, generally, to play the role of clown or buffoon. Such behaviors, of course, had the added function of reinforcing stereotypes of blacks as childlike and basically happy.

These more or less informal regulations over routine contacts were also reinforced, in the South, by many laws that restricted interactions in many public places, such as waiting rooms, swimming pools, parks, and restaurants. Blacks were placed in separate "Jim Crow" railway cars and were relegated to the back seats of buses. Rest rooms and drinking fountains were also segregated, with the quality of facilities assigned to blacks being noticeably inferior to (and cheaper than) those used by whites. All these patterns had the obvious function of drawing a very clear line between the two groups, a line that emphasized that the lowest-status white had many privileges that were closed to the highest-ranking black.

Although these ritualistic deference patterns may have given the impression to outsiders that relationships between blacks and whites in Southern communities were friendly and smooth-running, this does not imply that they were not backed by a number of mechanisms that ultimately relied on force. A black who acted "uppity", or seemed "surly" or "spoiled" by Yankee ways, was often marked for violence, with the ultimate threat of lynching being a vivid one in the memories of the older generation of blacks. Sometimes a black woman might get away with behavior that her male counterpart could never dare enact without fear of reprisals. But *all* blacks in these communities had to be on constant guard to control their impulses in any encounter with whites.[15] With members of their own group, however, it was a different story. As we have already noted, in-group aggression was tolerated by white law-enforcement officials as long as there was no threat to the white community.

These patterns within the South have now changed to a remarkable extent, though they have by no means disappeared, especially among the older generation of blacks. The Civil-Rights and black-power movements appear to have been largely responsible for this important change. During the 1960s white police for the first time found *themselves* in danger if they overstepped their authority, and today a white who insists on calling his black counterpart "boy" will at least have to consider the possibility of instant retaliation. As a result, interpersonal exchanges are much more egalitarian, though perhaps less overtly "friendly" and casual. Though it would be difficult to measure the effect accurately there has undoubtedly been a marked positive effect on black self-esteem.

In general, if the regulation of intergroup contacts is seen as an alternative to segregation in situations where segregation is not feasible, and if these regulations, themselves, begin to break down, we may anticipate one of two outcomes. Either the minority is on its way to becoming "integrated" into the larger social system, or the level of overt conflict between the two groups is likely to increase. In the following chapter our attention will be focused on power and conflict as key social processes that also must be taken into consideration in the study of racial and ethnic relations.

NOTES

1. The early "classic" on French Canada is Everett C. Hughes and Helen McGill Hughes, *French Canada in Transition* (University of Chicago Press, 1943). See also E. K. Francis, *Interethnic Relations,* chap. 11. Although French Canadians were technically migrants to the New World, their territorial claims go back several centuries and are directed toward English-speaking Canadians.

2. For discussions of indices of segregation and related methodological issues see especially Otis Dudley Duncan and Beverly Duncan, "A Methodological Analysis of Segregation Indexes," *American Sociological Review,* 20 (1955), pp. 210-217; and Karl E. Taeuber and Alma F. Taeuber, *Negroes in Cities* (Chicago: Aldine, 1965), appendix A.

3. Karl E. Taeuber and Alma F. Taeuber, *Negroes in Cities,* p. 37. These authors also report findings that show only very small changes in these scores during the decades 1940-1950, and 1950-1960. (Chicago: Aldine Publishing Co., 1965).

4. One of the reasons for the relatively lower segregation scores in the West may be the fact that the data are actually for nonwhites, rather than blacks, so that the relatively large numbers of Asian-Americans on the West Coast may deflate the figures for these cities.

5. See A. Sørensen, K. Taeuber, and L. Hollingsworth, "Indexes of Racial Residential Segregation for 109 Cities in the United States, 1940 to 1970." *Studies in Racial Segregation,* 1 (1974); see also, Reynolds Farley, "Residential Segregation and Its Implications for School Integration," *Law and Contemporary Problems,* 39 (Winter 1975), pp. 164-93.

6. The most thorough study of segregation among American ethnic minorities is Stanley Lieberson's *Ethnic Patterns in American Cities* (New York: Free Press, 1963). For a more recent study see A. M. Guest and J. A. Weed, "Ethnic Residential Segregation: Patterns of Change," *American Journal of Sociology,* 81 (1976), pp. 1088-1111.

7. See especially Luigi Laurenti, *Property Values and Race: Studies in Seven Cities* (Berkeley: University of California Press, 1960).

8. See H. M. Blalock, *Toward a Theory of Minority-Group Relations,* chap. 2.

9. Fredrik Barth, *Ethnic Groups and Boundaries.*

10. Gunnar Mydral, *An American Dilemma,* chap. 3.

11. Emory S. Bogardus, *Immigration and Race Attitudes* (New York: Heath, 1928).

12. See George E. Simpson and J. Milton Yinger, *Racial and Cultural Minorities: An Analysis of Prejudice and Discrimination,* 4th ed. (New York: Harper, 1972), chap. 5.

13. Gunnar Myrdal, *An American Dilemma,* pp. 40-42.

14. See Gunnar Myrdal, *An American Dilemma,* chap. 29; John Dollard, *Caste and Class in a Southern Town* (New York: Doubleday, 1949); and Charles S. Johnson, *Growing Up in the Black Belt* (Washington, D. C.: American Council on Education, 1941).

15. See John Dollard, *Caste and Class in a Southern Town;* Abram Kardiner and Lionel Ovesey, *The Mark of Oppression* (Cleveland: Meridian Books, 1962); and W. H. Grier and P. M. Cobbs, *Black Rage* (New York: Basic Books, 1968).

CHAPTER 7
POWER, CONFLICT, AND MINORITY REACTIONS

Racial and ethnic relations inherently are power contests between dominant and subordinate groups.[1] This is true even though these relationships may appear to be smooth-running and free of overt conflict. In fact, whenever power is very unevenly distributed among racial and ethnic groups, as it is in the United States, the minorities must necessarily accommodate themselves to situations that they would very much prefer to change if they had the resources to do so. It must therefore be recognized that power considerations are not linked in a simple fashion to the issue of whether or not there is overt conflict between two groups. In fact, conflict seems more likely whenever two groups are approximately evenly matched than in situations in which one group obviously dominates the other.

SOME BASIC CONCEPTS

The concept of "power" is an extremely broad one, though it has proven to be an elusive concept in the social sciences. In physics "power" is operationally defined as work accomplished per unit of time, so that the measurement of power depends on one's being able to isolate the impact of a single source of power, say an engine pulling on a lift, and then measuring its ability to accomplish a fixed amount of work in a given period of time. Power has both kinetic and potential aspects. "Kinetic power" refers to power in action, or work actually being accomplished, whereas "potential power" refers to the *ability* to accomplish this work under standardized conditions. If a machine or engine is constructed according to known principles, and then tested, we can safely assume that this potential will remain a constant (over some time span) and that others built like it will have approximately equal powers. In short, we have relatively simple ways of translating back and forth between power as potential and power in action; the machine "behaves" in accord with known laws, at least until it breaks down.

The concept of social power causes us more difficulty (even if we understand the similar distinction between "potential" and "kinetic" power). We recognize that the president of the United States, an army general, the chairman of the board of General Motors, or someone who owns several million dollars all have the *ability* to accomplish certain things by virtue of the positions they occupy or the properties they own. But there is a further distinction we must make. We must recognize the difference between these "objective" properties and positions, per se, and what we call "resources," or the sources of power potential. Neither position nor money, for example, constitutes an actual resource *unless* other actors have certain goals and beliefs. They must be willing to work for the money, or to carry out orders, and (usually) they must accept as legitimate the authority of the occupant of the position in question.

How power is actually exercised depends on two other factors in addition to resources. First, these resources will be mobilized to varying *degrees*. Resources will ordinarily be scarce and will need to be used for many different purposes. Even "authority" cannot be exercised too frequently if the cooperation of those upon whom it depends is needed on a continual basis. There will usually be some actors who believe that a given course of action is illegitimate, and the resistance that these actors mobilize will constitute an effective brake on the overuse of authority. If we define degree of power mobilization as the percentage of total resources actually used in a particular power confrontation, then the power exerted (P) will be roughly proportional to the total resources (R) times the degree of mobilization (M).

Second, not all courses of action will be equally *efficient*. Money may be spent for a number of different courses of action, some being more wasteful than others. Or a minority may support two distinct courses of action that have the net effect of cancelling each other out. Sometimes technical knowledge is needed to help ascertain the most efficient means of action, and if this knowledge is not obtainable the course selected may be much less efficient than others that might have been used. Thus efficiency will depend upon such factors as degree of coordination and consensus among different segments of a group, the availability of knowledge, and the normative system under which a group is operating. Sometimes, for example, means that would be most efficient are ruled out for religious or ethical reasons or because there are strong cultural taboos against their use.

In physics "efficiency" is measured in terms of the ratio of output to input energy. Although the measurement of efficiency would be much more complicated in the social sciences, we all recognize that efficiency must be taken into consideration in estimating the effective power that is actually being put into practice. Roughly, we may multiply efficiency (E) by resources (R) and degree of mobilization (*M*), so that power exerted will be approximately proportional to the product of these three factors (that is, P=kERM, where k is a constant). The implication of this formula is that the absence of any *one* of the three terms will produce a near zero amount of exerted power. Thus, without the necessary resources, no degree of mobilization or efficiency will matter. But by the same token, if efficiency is near zero, neither resources nor a high degree of mobilization will help.

Relating this power formula to our earlier discussion of *utilities* (goal values) and *subjective probabilities* (likelihoods of actions achieving desired goals), we note that mobilization may be low for either or both of two reasons: (1) there may be virtually no utility attached to changing the situation or exerting power, or (2) the subjective probability of achieving the desired change may be exceedingly low. Suppose, for example, that whites observe that blacks appear to be "accepting" the status quo without attempting to change it. Perhaps blacks like the system as it is—a convenient thing for members of the dominant group to believe. If so, lack of black mobilization for change would be due to a near zero *utility* for change. What is far more likely, however, is that blacks do not believe they can possibly change the system, or that efforts to produce a change will be exceedingly costly to them in other ways. If so, then their *subjective probability* of achieving a desired change will be near zero.

Recall that we argued that the expected level of behavior—here conceived as "mobilization"—will also be a multiplicative effect of subjective probabilities and utilities. If we assume that the subjective probabilities, in turn, will be partly a function of the minority's relative *resources*, then their mobilization (*M*) will also be a function of these resources. Thus a minority that has been in a subordinate position and that wishes to change this situation will be expected to increase its exerted power roughly in proportion to the *square* of its resources, if we assume that *M* will also be proportional to these resources.[2] It is no wonder, then, that dominant groups are often obsessed with the need to prevent potentially powerful minorities from gaining any new resources at the expense of the dominant group.

Dominant-group power mobilization, in contrast, is often kept at a low level because of indifference. This is especially true for numerically small minorities that have little or no relevance for the overwhelming majority of the dominant group. If, for instance, there are very few profitable exchanges with the minority, and if only a small fraction of the dominant group are in direct competition with the minority, then there may be few *economic* gains from discrimination. Members of the dominant group, however, may continue to avoid the minority for status reasons, or perhaps because of a belief that these contacts would be unpleasant. The predominant orientation may therefore be that of convenient ignorance. The minority is simply not a conspicuous factor in the day-to-day living of majority individuals, but by the same token there is also no real support for programs designed to assist such a minority.

Under such circumstances, a relatively weak minority faces a number of important dilemmas with respect to strategy. If it attempts to call itself to the attention of the dominant group, this may indeed arouse sympathy and a degree of support for reforms of a noncontroversial nature. This appears to have been precisely the kind of support induced during the early stages of the Civil Rights movement, at least with respect to Northern support for civil-rights legislation directed primarily at the South. But more dramatic protest demonstrations, particularly those that tended to produce a fear reaction among whites or that demanded much more substantial monetary sacrifices, may have served to increase white mobilization against blacks. Since a dominant group may remain more or less dormant, with a very low degree of mobilization, while maintaining its power advantage as a result of its overwhelming superiority of resources, from the minority perspective the trick is to gain support from a sufficiently large segment of this majority without at the same time mobilizing the forces of opposition.

From the standpoint of this particular strategic dilemma we may distinguish between two very different types of minority resources. First, there are what we have referred to as "competitive resources," which ordinarily accrue to individual members of a minority and which enable them to *reward* at least some segments of the dominant group. For instance, if minority members possess certain special job skills that make them especially desirable to employers, or if they are believed to be unusually good neighbors, these traits may give these individuals an edge over other competitors, or at least a compensation for their minority handicaps.

A minority that stresses the importance of attaining such competitive resources, we suspect, is also very likely to place a heavy emphasis on the conformity to dominant-group practices and the desirability of working toward an integrationist solution to the minority problem. The Japanese-American "success story" is perhaps our best illustration of this particular minority strategy. A somewhat more mixed case is that of the Jewish minority, since it also stresses additional patterns that imply a somewhat more pluralistic orientation. The essential point about competitive resources, however, is that they permit *individuals* to compete on approximately equal terms with members of the dominant group.

The second type of resource, which may take a number of different forms, we will call "pressure resources."[3] This term refers to resources that enable the minority, or its coalition partners, to apply pressure in the form of threatened punishments. For instance, a minority may be able to get the federal government to withhold contracts from employers who do not employ a sufficient number of minority members or who practice discriminatory promotion policies. Or the minority may attempt to organize boycotts, as for example those that occurred during the Civil Rights movements in many Southern communities or those that have been organized by Cesar Chavez and the United Farm Workers against the grape, lettuce, and wine industries in California.[4]

These pressure tactics, of course, may be used to improve the competitive resources of the minority. For example the many protest movements that oc-curred on college campuses during the 1960s resulted in vastly increased numbers of minority students and faculty being admitted to these schools. Pressure re-sources, which for the most part rely on threats of punishment, may be very ef-fective, but their mobilization also requires a higher degree of surveillance and coordination for this same reason. Basically, since they do not rely on positive incentives or rewards, they do not have the immediate effect of stimulating the cooperation of the target agency, though eventually a common understanding may be reached. For instance, where the threat comes primarily from the federal government, with its recognized power to withhold funds or initiate judicial ac-tion, the pressure may achieve a more or less permanent effect without constant surveillance. But in many instances, without a sustained pressure there will be a tendency to lapse back to the original level of discrimination once the pressure has been reduced.

The use of these pressure resources also has the attendant risk of genera-ting a "backlash" effect, through which the superior resources of the dominant group are mobilized in opposition. This gives rise to the possibility of increasing overt conflict involving the exchange of negative sanctions or punishments. As one group escalates in the use of such punishment tactics, we may expect the other to do likewise unless there are counterforces that make this mutual in-crease in hostilities level off.

MINORITY REACTIONS
TO DOMINANT-GROUP POWER

Since we have defined minorities to be those racial, ethnic, or possibly other social groupings that are in a subordinate position, regardless of their nu-merical size, then it is true by definition that minorities will tend to be in rela-tively weak power positions vis-a-vis the majority or dominant group. But some minorities are much stronger than others, and in fact some will be in a position to extract important concessions from the dominant group, particularly if they can locate coalition partners with which they may cooperate. Thus minorities will have a number of options available to them, with the viability of the alterna-tives depending on the nature of the resources they possess, the degree and effi-ciency with which they can mobilize these resources, and the availability of coa-lition partners. Not all of these alternatives will be mutually compatible, how-ever, and we may also anticipate that some members of a minority will choose one alternative whereas others will select very different ones.

We may begin this section by noting four very broad classes of alternatives that are open to a minority and its individual members. First, the minority may attempt to disappear as a distinct group, assuming its members can "pass" as members of the majority or that their minority status can lose its conspicuous-ness or relevance to members of the dominant group. Second, the minority may attempt to isolate or insulate itself from most contacts with the majority or—as an individualistic counterpart to this strategy—its individual members may attempt to "escape" from important encounters with the majority. Third, the minority may attempt to find a coalition partner or partners, thereby pooling resources in order to gain power in relation to the majority. Finally, the minority may, itself, engage in a power struggle with the dominant group, without benefit of coalition partners.

Each of these alternative strategies will have subjective probabilities of success that will vary with the circumstances, and we would expect that many minorities will vacillate among these alternatives or be split into factions that attempt differing solutions. An extremely weak and numerically small minority can hardly hope to succeed via either of the last two alternatives, and neither will it make a very attractive coalition partner given its very small amount of power.[5] Thus we would expect such a minority to attempt either of the first two strategies, perhaps alternating among them. A somewhat stronger minority may be in a position to attempt the coalition strategy as well, particularly if there are several other similar minorities available or if the dominant group is divided on other issues. A numerically large but currently weak minority, as for example blacks in South Africa, may be in a much stronger position to attempt the fourth strategy, or perhaps to combine it with a temporary coalition with an outside power, as for example a neighboring country.

In the case of all four alternatives, however, it needs to be stressed that the minority cannot act "rationally" without paying close attention to the expected reactions on the part of the dominant group, and in this sense its behaviors must be considered as heavily dependent on what the dominant group stands to gain and lose. A minority that is needed to provide cheap labor, which cannot be supplied by any other source, is in a very different position from one that is merely in the way or whose services have become redundant. Similarly, a minority whose culture threatens the way of life of the majority is quite different from one that deviates in only a few minor ways.

Attempting the first two alternatives simultaneously as a group solution, appears very difficult, although it may very well be possible for some minority *individuals* to pass or assimilate into the larger society, whereas others attempt to escape. A group-oriented withdrawal process, or what amounts to a separatist movement, typically requires tight control over one's members, a series of socialization practices that inhibit members of the younger generation from moving toward the dominant group, and—usually—some territorial base the integrity of which can be protected from majority infiltration. If too many members of any given generation attempt to integrate or assimilate, then obviously the basis of a separatist movement will be dissipated.

It may be possible, however, to eject those dissident members who prefer to lose their minority identity, though this often must be done in a very dramatic fashion. Otherwise, their later return may serve to undermine the distinctive minority culture that is necessary to maintain the separatist movement. For example, many American Indian tribes have had to face the dilemma of how to deal with those members who have migrated to the city and become partly "white" in orientation but who do not wish to cut off tribal ties altogether. Too great a proportion of such marginal members will, of course, produce major generational strains as well as a tendency to look down upon those features of the Native American culture that appear "backward" and nonfunctional in an industrial society.

Prior to the reemphasis on blackness that occurred during the Civil Rights movement of the 1960s, many blacks engaged in almost frantic efforts to become more white. Those very few who could actually pass for white sometimes attempted to do so, with considerable guilt and fear of being detected. Others placed a premium on fair complexions, hair-straightening devices, and various cosmetics designed to make the individual appear much less dark. A light skin color was associated with higher status within black communities, and often a lighter-skinned child was favored over his or her darker siblings.[6] One can hardly imagine a more frustrating and psychologically degrading process, as well as one that was obviously doomed to failure.

A more realistic resolution, where the dominant group permits it, is that of attempting to compensate for one's skin color or minority status by obtaining competitive resources that are valued by members of the dominant majority. Thus black athletes, musicians, and actors have, for several decades now, been able to "make it" into reasonably elite circles, as has the occasional black political leader. Many Jews have likewise achieved high status as a result of intellectual, artistic, or business talents, thus in large part overcoming the degree of prejudice that still exists. A basic problem with this minority strategy, however, is that the vast majority of minority members do not achieve these high success levels and therefore do not find this resolution a viable alternative. To some degree, however, they do gain through two mechanisms, namely, through a kind of vicarious enjoyment in seeing members of their own group succeed and also by virtue of the fact that each additional success of one of their members makes it just a bit easier to overcome future barriers and just a bit harder for the majority to hold on to negative minority stereotypes.

The American "success story" among racial minorities is that of Japanese-Americans, who have become almost fully accepted during the relatively brief thirty-five-year span since their release from U. S. internment camps during the 1940s. Although it has been stressed that second-generation (Nisei) Japanese-Americans may have paid a psychic price in terms of repressed impulses in conforming to middle-class behavioral norms, there can be no doubt that this strategy has paid off handsomely in terms of their educational, occupational, and income levels that closely approximate those of whites (and even exceed them in terms of educational levels). The researcher Harry Kitano points out that, in addition to a strong family system that emphasizes conformity to middle-class standards, Japanese culture also places a heavy emphasis on displays of humility and politeness, which also undoubtedly helped create an image of Japanese-

Americans as "nice people" and good neighbors whose children were nearly always well behaved, hard working, and yet not "pushy" or overly aggressive.[7]

Thus although Japanese-Americans and Jews have played somewhat similar roles, occupationally, the former minority has also succeeded in avoiding many of the negative stereotypes that often accompany those who appear to be a bit too competitive or ambitious. It may very well be true that these second-generation Japanese-Americans have paid a price, as individuals, by inhibiting their more aggressive impulses and by overconforming to middle-class standards, but it also seems evident that their children have reaped important benefits. It remains to be seen whether members of these later generations may relax from some of the more rigid standards of their parents, while still being accepted into middle-class society. Thus far, this appears to be the case. If so, Japanese-Americans may become the first racially distinct minority to "make it" into the great American "melting pot" along with most of our white ethnic minorities.

From the standpoint of minorities, one unfortunate possibility is that majority policies may fluctuate for reasons that are entirely outside of minority control. As we have already noted, European Jews from time to time have come close to full assimilation in their host societies, with intermarriage rates being sufficiently high that many persons of mixed parentage have not even been aware of their Jewish heritage. Then suddenly, perhaps because of economic depression or labor unrest, they find themselves targeted as scapegoats, with the result that in-group loyalties and segregation become critical as protective mechanisms. This, indeed, was the fate of millions of Jews under the Nazi regime, but it would be a mistake to consider this particular tragedy as historically unique.

William Wilson has noted that blacks have alternated between integrationist and separatist philosophies, depending upon their degree of optimism concerning their acceptance in the larger white society.[8] During times of moderate to rapid progress, the integrationist approach has prevailed, whereas when progress has slowed down (relative to expectation levels) there has been a much more pronounced tendency to turn toward separatism. Needless to say, minorities may not always adjust rapidly to these fluctuations in their external environment, so that there will inevitably be lags in their responses as well as sharp disagreements as to the best strategy to follow.

As implied earlier, many minority individuals may attempt a withdrawal strategy even in instances where others of their group are moving toward integration and the achievement of competitive resources. Often, we label these efforts to withdraw as "escape mechanisms," but they are really nothing more than efforts to cope with a very difficult situation. Unfortunately for the individuals concerned, however, many such coping mechanisms are maladaptive and in effect force the individual into deeper and deeper withdrawal patterns. Drug addiction and alcoholism are two obvious patterns of this type, with both tending to isolate the individual more and more from members of his or her own group. The stereotype of the "Skid Road" Indian, hopelessly alcoholic and friendless, comes to mind. But there are other more social types of escape mechanisms that are also possible: the person who spends endless days hanging around the pool hall, the ardent television addict, the petty gambler, the prostitute and pimp, and those who attempt to gain solace by joining a religious cult that engulfs their entire emotional and intellectual lives. Such religious forms of escape are sometimes especially welcomed by a dominant group as mechanisms for draining off minority frustrations in harmless directions.

A basic organizational dilemma faced by minorities is whether or not to encourage the development of competitive resources that attach to individuals; choosing to do so may have the effect of encouraging the more successful of its members from dissociating themselves from those members who have not been able to compete successfully. In particular, the gap between these elite minority members and those who have, in effect, given up and turned to individualistic escape mechanisms may become quite severe. The latter constitute a source of embarrassment for the former who, in turn, are regarded as traitors to the minority. There is an interesting series of terms all of which make fun of the integrationist-oriented minority individual who appears to be "colored" on the outside but has really surrendered to "whiteness" on the inside: "oreos" (in the case of blacks), "bananas" (for Asian-Americans), "apples" (for Indians), and "coconuts" (for Chicanos). It may in fact be exceedingly difficult for a minority to stimulate in-group loyalties while simultaneously encouraging its members to succeed in the larger dominant social system. At the same time, it may also be difficult to provide protective mechanisms for those who fail in such a system.

COALITIONS AMONG MINORITIES

Whenever there are a reasonable number of medium-sized minorities, the "rational" course of action would seem to be for these minorities to form a coalition with one another. Yet truly effective coalitions among minorities seem to be rather rare, and so it becomes important to discover the conditions that seem to inhibit or encourage coalition formation. In particular, if minorities are not in mutual contact, have very diverse cultures and economic interests, and have had a previous history of intense competition or conflict with one another, then one may expect that the degree of mutual trust and communication among them will be too low to overcome the normal resistances to cooperation.

Many minorities that are conveniently lumped together and considered to be single minorities by outsiders—groups such as American Indians and Hispanics—are really very loose-knit and sometimes ineffective coalitions of much smaller groups. This fact does suggest, however, that rudimentary coalitions among minorities are reasonably frequent and likely to be based on several structural factors, such as degree of similarity among minority groupings, extensiveness of contact and numbers of "bridging personnel," degree of hierarchicization among minorities, and economic specialization.

The nature of previous contact between any two potential coalition partners will affect two factors: the degree of trust between them, and, as a consequence, the degree to which they anticipate they can mobilize effectively together. Where there have been extensive friendly contacts and, especially, intermarriage between two (or more) minorities, we also expect that there will be a relatively large proportion of "bridging personnel," who can play leadership roles in the coalition. Likewise, if the groups have not been in extensive competition for land, jobs, or other scarce resources, and yet have had a reasonable degree of previous contact with one another, this should also facilitate coalition formation, not only by increasing the trust factor but also by increasing the chances that the two parties can agree on a joint course of action that does not benefit one party at the expense of the other.

Closely related to previous minority contact and competition is the question of how the minorities are ranked along some relatively distinct hierarchy of prestige or power. This, too, is likely to be linked to whatever are the predominant lines of social cleavage within the society. Where there are multiple lines of cleavage—say, economic, linguistic, religious, and regional—it is highly unlikely that the minorities can be arranged neatly in any single hierarchy that is clearcut and obvious to the members of each group.

If, however, social groups are obviously hierarchically arranged—as in the case of the ideal type caste system—we can predict that in such settings coalitions among minorities are rather unlikely.[9] A given minority may wish to join with another minority that is somewhat higher than itself but will tend to reject those lower down in the hierarchy, and this will most likely result in what Theodore Caplow refers to as a "conservative" coalition. If, for example, groups A, B, C, and D are hierarchically arranged, with A superior to B, B superior to C, and so on, then if D were to challenge C, or C and D to challenge B, those higher in the hierarchy would be likely to step in to preserve the arrangement. Of course, if A is relatively strong as compared with all three, and if B, C, and D begin to struggle to change their relative positions, A may simply play off each against the others with the intent of weakening all three, or at least sewing the seeds of distrust among them.

Insofar as relative minority size is directly related to position in the hierarchy, we may apply the same kind of argument to relationships among minorities of different sizes. In the interesting case where, say, minority D is much larger than C but lower in the hierarchy, there will be added incentive for C to join forces conservatively with A and B in order to keep D in its place.

Degree of similarity to the dominant group is also likely to be a strong correlate of position in the hierarchy. If C is more similar to A and B than is D, C will have a vested interest in emphasizing its differences with D and its similarities with B. But B, in turn, will wish to distinguish itself from C (as well as D) and to emphasize its similarity to A. A, in turn is likely to differentiate itself from all three minorities unless, of course, it finds it necessary from time to time to form a conservative coalition with B against C and D, or with B and C against D.

"Middleman" minorities, as well as mixed-blood populations, often find themselves in positions such as B and C in this example.[10] They may be able to form temporary coalitions with more elite groups when they are needed, but later they are likely to find themselves isolated when the danger of a revolutionary coalition (among lower-ranking minorities) has subsided. If it is possible for a group such as A to use B or C as a temporary scapegoat to drain off D's hostility, then in effect A and D may form a coalition of sorts against these intermediate groups, though it is unlikely that A will permit the destruction of B or C as long as the hierarchical arrangement is useful to it in preserving stability. Over time, however, it is possible that B may merge with A, or perhaps C with B, thereby shortening the hierarchical chain.

Apart from hierarchical orderings, minorities may be to varying degrees in direct economic competition with one another. Often, of course, "competition" is difficult to pinpoint precisely or to measure, but the *perceived* competition may be real nevertheless. Most important, perhaps, is the extent to which the minorities perceive themselves to be in a "zero-sum" competition in which the gains of one group must always be made at the expense of another. On the other hand, minorities may perceive themselves as being in a "positive-sum" situation in which the gains of one add to the gains of all, making a coalition more desirable.

Many minorities throughout the world are oriented toward isolating or insulating themselves from the larger society, if not toward ultimate separation from it. What implications does such an orientation have for coalition formation? First, to the degree that a minority is really successful in isolating or insulating itself, this will obviously close off contacts with other minorities that are attempting a similar strategy. Such groups may *imitate* each other—as appears to have been the case with respect to the tactics of many mutually isolated American Indian tribes—but genuine coordination of behaviors becomes highly unlikely. If, however, such minorities are able to "send out" a sufficient number of their members to the outside world, but at the same time these persons remain motivated to help retain these insulative mechanisms, the probability of mutual collaboration becomes much greater. To some extent, this pattern may be developing among leaders of American Indian tribal organizations.

It is difficult, however, to imagine how groups can socialize their members to prefer insulation without, at the same time, instilling in them a basic fear and distrust of outsiders, including other minorities. This is all the more true if there has been a previous history of mutually hostile contact. Given such fear and distrust, we would expect that any efforts to establish coalitions will be short lived and that, unless the coalition achieves quick and dramatic victories, it will involve major leadership struggles, disagreements over priorities, and highly inefficient organizational structures. All of this can be expected to affect adversely both the degree and efficiency of mobilization, as well as the basic trust among partners. For these reasons we would predict a very low success rate of coalitions among minorities having these objectives, as well as between a minority wishing to insulate itself and a second minority that has assimilation among its objectives.

CONFLICT AND AGGRESSION AS MINORITY STRATEGIES

There is probably more hypocrisy surrounding the notion of violence and conflict than any other subject, including sex. The reasons are rather easy to understand. The use of violence in interpersonal and intergroup relations is *both* highly instrumental and terribly risky. Furthermore, in-group aggression is either highly ritualized (and nondangerous) or severely sanctioned. The world's major religions all are opposed to killing (though this of course has not in any way limited extreme cruelty and warfare in the name of religious ideologies).

In practically all social systems, violence is legitimated by means of an ideological system that justifies its use under specified circumstances and provides rationalizations for at least those forms of violence and conflict that are functional to group interests and survival. Thus killing enemies in warfare may earn one a medal of honor.

Violence against minorities has on occasion stirred the consciences of an aroused public, but much more often it has either gone totally unnoticed or else has been justified as a means of control. As noted earlier, it was not until the slave trade became unprofitable to the British that the numerous deaths resulting from this form of commerce suddenly became a subject for serious debate. For several decades during the late 1800s and early 1900s blacks were routinely lynched in the South, sometimes with the active participation of law-enforcement authorities. Virtually none of the guilty parties were punished, and this form of social control was legitimated as a device to make the South safe for white womanhood and to help keep "uppity" blacks in their place.

More recently, minorities in America still find themselves victims of police brutality.[11] A disproportionate percentage of minority members are targets of police shootings. In 1979 the U. S. Department of Justice took the extreme step of charging Philadelphia's police force with brutality against blacks and Hispanics, though (for some reason) it subsequently dropped the charges. But the federal government has, itself, also been deeply involved in minority harrassment. Perhaps the most notable incident to come to light was the FBI's effort to pressure Martin Luther King, Jr. into committing suicide on the eve of his receiving the Nobel Peace Prize. Although the FBI has not been directly linked to the King assassination, there are many blacks who—in view of the FBI's known hostility to King—still believe that it was, at least, implicated. There have been similar suspicions of FBI involvement in the police slayings of several Black Panther leaders in Chicago. This federal agency also has had numerous conflicts with militant American Indian leaders, and one may be almost positive that violence associated with the militants was not entirely their fault. In short, police violence in

America is still a potent means of minority control. Needless to say it also serves as a major irritant within minority communities, as the number of minority demands for police accountability and civilian-review boards clearly indicates.

Thus violence and conflict are part and parcel of minority-group relations, even though they may be relatively rare during periods of "normalcy." The hypocrisy occurs, however, when members of dominant groups cry foul play whenever minorities threaten violence or attempt to resort to much milder forms of conflict, such as boycotts, street marches, the taking over of campus buildings, and the like. Under such circumstances dominant groups often refuse to negotiate with minorities, claiming they will not respond to threats. Appeals to law and order and due process may also be made, even in instances where the majority vote and the judicial system are clearly invoking policies counter to the minority's interests. It is no wonder, then, that many of these minority members become cynical about not only the police and other law-enforcement agents but our entire system of justice.

Most minorities cannot afford to engage in conflict, however, for a very simple reason: they are not sufficiently powerful and must guard against the natural tendency to overreact, which might risk even greater violence on the part of the dominant majority. Most acts of violence on both sides will be rather rare and will be carried out by a small segment of the population. Many persons, however, will secretly endorse if not actually support those who engage in such retaliatory acts. Official violence by representatives of a legitimate government may be met by varying degrees of guerrilla warfare, sometimes involving police slayings but usually involving much safer forms of aggression that will be condoned by most members of the minority community.

The use of violence and open guerrilla warfare probably makes sense as a minority strategy in situations where the dominant group is actually a numerical minority and where it no longer has strong economic incentives for maintaining dominance over the minority. The type of guerrilla movement espoused by the revolutionary Frantz Fanon was ideally suited to Algeria (about which Fanon wrote) and other African territories where the ruling colonial powers were finding it increasingly costly to hold on to areas that were worth more as symbols of a past colonial era than as economic assets.[12] Here, terrorism and conflict contributed considerably to the fatigue of the colonial powers, so much so that they were willing to abandon the interests of the small minority of white settlers. In effect, the coalitions that existed between these white-settler groups and the colonial powers broke down because the punishments being handed out to the latter were far greater than the rewards.

Similar patterns of violence also took place in what used to be called French Indochina, where the United States inherited a continuation of this war of independence in the form of the Vietnamese civil war. Ultimately, we too became exhausted and pulled out, as did the Portuguese in Angola and Mozambique. The British, on the whole, were much wiser (as were the Dutch and Belgians) in handling the break up of their former colonial holdings. There is no doubt, however, that the threat of continued conflict, combined with the diminished value of these territories, were primarily responsible for the establishment of most of the new nations of Africa and South Asia. Guerrilla warfare has also finally led to the overthrow of white dominance in Rhodesia (now Zimbabwe).

Most internal minorities, however, are in a far different situation since the initiation of conflict is likely to invite a degree of retaliation that results in a higher degree of repression than previously existed. Minorities that are sufficiently large or that have enough resources to enable them to become a useful coalition partner also have the problem of limiting their actions to ones which that partner will find acceptable. (This was one of the difficulties that plagued the loose-knit coalition between blacks and white liberals during the Civil Rights movement of the 1960s, and this ultimately led to a rebellion on the part of a relatively small number of black-power extremists.) Furthermore, conflict strategy, once implemented, is difficult to control, since the opposing side is likely to use retaliatory means that produce an accelerating momentum, often involving the increasing use of violence. Each act by one side calls for a rejoinder on the part of the other, with both sides conveniently denying their own past actions that have helped to produce the acceleration in hostilities. A minority that is only moderately large and that does not have reliable allies is simply not in a position to absorb the resulting escalating punishment from a dominant group.

Moderate degrees of conflict—possibly including some mild forms of violence—often may have symbolic importance to a minority that has continually been the victim of aggression. Retaliatory aggression also has the consequence of inhibiting many forms of spontaneous aggression on the part of the dominant group. The race riots that took place in Chicago, Detroit, and several other cities immediately after World War I, as well as the riots during World War II, served notice on the white population that blacks intended to fight back when attacked. Significantly enough, there have been no subsequent riots that have involved masses of white participants. The urban disturbances of the 1960s, in contrast, pitted black participants against predominantly white police and national guardsmen. The latter, too, learned from these riots that unless one exercised a certain amount of caution in making arrests or in calming tempers, one's own life might very well be in danger.

Unfortunately, many of these later-day conflicts turned into what some social scientists have termed "police riots," during which law-enforcement officers sometimes shot indiscriminately into crowds or engaged in needless beatings.[13] Thus the major lesson that may have been learned, by some police officials, is that aggression against minorities may be dangerous *unless* it can be accomplished without witnesses and under the protection of large numbers of other officials. On the whole, however, violence toward blacks appears to have subsided considerably, especially within the South. A retaliatory mood especially among the younger black urban population has undoubtedly had its chilling effect on would-be white aggressors.

A degree of overt conflict also appears to have been largely responsible for dramatic changes on many college campuses, which for the most part contained only a handful of blacks and other minorities prior to the Civil Rights disturbances. Earlier, peaceful efforts to persuade college administrators to admit more minorities, to hire minority faculty, and to institute special programs for minorities typically fell on deaf ears. But with the onset of campus uprisings, takeovers of administration buildings, and very explicit demands made by black militants and radical white students, many colleges abruptly responded with long-needed reforms of black admissions, hirings, and other related problems.

Perhaps a mixed strategy is the optimal one for most minorities. The nonviolent protest movement of the late 1950s and early 1960s, which involved a number of conflict tactics of a rather mild nature, was especially effective. When these nonviolent tactics succeeded in provoking a violent reaction on the part of some Southern law-enforcement officers, and when national television brought these acts to the attention of millions of viewers who had no vested interests in these communities, an almost immediate coalition was formed between liberal whites (including political leaders) and these black protesters.

It is difficult to maintain a sense of political urgency without accelerating one's demands and actions, however, and thus the black minority was posed with a serious dilemma that ultimately proved the undoing of the coalition and its social movement. But if the gains of such a movement can be consolidated, then a later period of reduction in tensions and conflict, during which improved understandings can take place, appears to be a much more productive state of affairs than one in which hostilities continue to escalate into the kind of open guerrilla warfare that has taken place in Northern Ireland during the past decade.

What remains to be seen is what the white majority in America will do when faced with long-run economic problems of a very serious nature, including a possible drop in its average standard of living. Will it be willing to tolerate any substantial protest movements of the type that occurred during the relatively prosperous decade of the 1960s? The fatigue factor, in the case of the white majority, appears to have been due primarily to indifference and the lack of a strong vested interest in holding blacks down. If unemployment mounts, however, and if a growing proportion of middle-class families find it necessary to have two breadwinners to keep up with inflation, and if the opposition to welfare programs and taxes also mounts, this indifference may be turned to hostility. In this case the tolerance for minority protest may turn into a tolerance for extreme forms of aggression aimed at preventing such protests. If so, we may see precisely the kind of open guerrilla warfare that has proven so disruptive in other parts of the world.

NOTES

1. A more theoretical treatment, using the same basic concepts, is given in Blalock and Wilken, *Intergroup Processes,* chaps. 8 and 9.

2. If we assume that $P = kERM$, and that $M = a + bR$, then $P = kER(a + bR) = akER + bkER^2$. For the portion of this parabola with which we are concerned, the exerted power will thus not only increase with R but the rate of increase will be an

accelerating one. This suggests that minorities that are already reasonably powerful will mobilize their resources to a greater degree than weaker minorities, provided that there are still inequities in the system that they wish to modify.

3. H. M. Blalock, *Toward a Theory of Minority-Group Relations,* chap. 4.

4. For discussions of the United Farm Workers movement see Julian Nava (ed.), *Viva La Raza!* (New York: Van Nostrand, 1973), part 5. See also Wayne Moquin and Charles Van Doren (eds.), *A Documentary History of the Mexican Americans* (New York: Bantam Books, 1971), part 5.

5. Several theories of coalition formation predict that if there are three parties *A, B,* and *C,* with *A* more powerful than *B* and *B* more powerful than *C,* then *B* and *C* are likely to form a coalition against *A* if the combined power of *B* and *C* is greater than that of *A.* No coalition is likely, however, if the powers of *B* and *C* together are less than that of *A.* See especially Theodore Caplow, *Two Against One* (Englewood Cliffs, N.J.: Prentice-Hall, 1968); and William A. Gamson, "A Theory of Coalition Formation," *American Sociological Review* 26 (1961), pp. 373–82. The "classic" sociological theorist who dealt with coalitions was Georg Simmel. See Lewis Coser (ed.), *Georg Simmel* (Englewood Cliffs, N.J.: Prentice-Hall, 1965).

6. See, for example, Kardiner and Ovesey, *The Mark of Oppression;* E. Franklin Frazier, *Black Bourgeoisie;* and Gunnar Myrdal, *An American Dilemma,* chap. 32.

7. Harry H. L. Kitano, *Japanese Americans: The Evolution of a Subculture* (Englewood Cliffs, N.J.: Prentice-Hall, 1969), especially chaps. 5 and 7. As implied by the subtitle of this book, however, Kitano suggests that Japanese-Americans are developing a distinct subculture, though one that is highly compatible with middle-class American values.

8. William J. Wilson, *Power, Racism, and Privilege: Race Relations in Theoretical and Sociohistorical Perspectives* (New York: Macmillan, 1973), chap. 4.

9. Theodore Caplow, *Two Against One,* chap. 5. Caplow's discussion is primarily in terms of hierarchical arrangements within organizations, but the argument appears to generalize to coalitions among minorities as well.

10. See H. M. Blalock, *Toward a Theory of Minority-Group Relations,* chap. 3.

11. See the *Report of the National Advisory Commission on Civil Disorders* (New York: Bantam Books, 1968). See also Jerome H. Skolnick, *The Politics of Protest* (New York: Ballantine Books, 1969).

12. See Frantz Fanon, *The Wretched of the Earth* (New York: Grove Press, 1963).

13. See Rodney Stark, *Police Riots: Collective Violence and Law Enforcement* (New York: Wadsworth, 1972).

CHAPTER 8
SOME POLICY
IMPLICATIONS

The social scientist's primary role is to study social phenomena as carefully and objectively as possible, always keeping an open mind about alternative explanations or new data that may undermine existing theories. But having attempted to analyze social reality without unnecessary oversimplifications, the social scientist is then left with nagging ethical or moral concerns that also need to be faced. Or at least *someone* will be faced with these problems even though a particular social scientist may elect to leave policy matters to others.

In this introductory work we have just begun to scratch the surface, and the reader will need to delve much more deeply into the subject before evaluating these issues from the standpoint of social action. There are a number of disturbing questions, however, that probably have already occurred to the reader. It seems wise to raise a few of these explicitly before considering their policy implications.

First, it is clear that racial and ethnic problems are not peculiar to any one region of the world. They have been intensified during the past two hundred years, however, as a result of the dramatic expansion of nationalism and large-scale capitalistic enterprises. One may wonder, then, whether there can ever be a system in which distinct racial and ethnic groups can gain sufficient freedom from dominance so that the discrimination and exploitation of the past will not be repeated. Are we doomed to an endless future of intergroup conflicts, not only among nation-states but within them as well?

Second, no one can seriously question that in the past capitalism has been responsible for arrangements involving the extensive inequitable use of slaves, serfs, contract laborers, and cheap industrial labor. Our own capitalist system has also accommodated to pressures from majority-group workers to discriminate against minorities. Unemployment rates among blacks and other low-status minorities are very high, especially among younger workers in our largest metropolitan areas. Is there any reason to believe that the situation for these minorities will inevitably improve? What are the mechanisms, if any, under which a capitalist economy "corrects" for such inequities?

Third, are there any better alternatives to this system? Have socialist governments been any less prone to selecting minorities as scapegoats or to relegating them to society's least desirable roles? The fact that we have been prevented, through secrecy, from studying antiminority policies in the Soviet Union, China, Vietnam, or Cambodia does not afford grounds for optimism. Can a totalitarian socialist government operate without suppressing religious or politically deviant minorities?

Fourth, to what extent are racial and ethnic cleavages simply a manifestation of "human nature?" If any particular cleavage among groups ceases to exist, will it simply be replaced by others because of psychological needs to aggress against some target or to take advantage of whatever parties happen to be the most vulnerable? If we attempt to control discriminatory behaviors toward one minority, will they simply be transferred to others? And if a present minority were to turn the tables and become dominant, would it not merely repeat the behaviors that had been applied to itself?

Fifth, will there ever be a sufficient proportion of majority-group members who become concerned enough to support sustained prominority policies, unless it is clearly in their own interests to do so? What does it take to overcome "convenient ignorance" or indifference? Is it inevitable that reform efforts will be confined to token programs that involve minimal costs and controversy? Can minorities ever count on majority-group members as active coalition partners in large enough numbers to assure continued change in their favor? Or will they be deserted in times of crisis or whenever support becomes too costly?

Finally, in a democracy based on majority rule can we construct truly effective mechanisms for protecting minorities from infringements on their civil rights? Can we assure ourselves that there will not be subtle—but perfectly legal— devices used to place these minorities at a severe economic disadvantage? How can persons who are weak in terms of economic and political power protect themselves against an organized majority that chooses to keep them in this position?

If all these questions are decidedly pessimistic ones, it is simply to emphasize that the problems we face are extremely difficult ones. Prejudice, discrimination, aggression, and hatred are not merely relics of the past. They exist today and can increase dramatically at any moment. A sudden depression brought about by an energy crisis, a continued high rate of inflation coupled with demands to reduce services to the needy, an international crisis, or the rise of a demagogic leader could set off the spark. Nor is open warfare among extremist groups beyond imagination, and once started it could be very difficult to bring under control. Thus it would be unwise to assume that racial and ethnic tensions will somehow steadily and inevitably heal by themselves. It is utterly unrealistic to believe that minority problems throughout the world will uniformly improve or that Americans will be unaffected by these outside events.

Whenever one is confronted by disturbing questions involving complex issues, the temptation is to put them off. There is little cause for optimism that "normal" political processes will solve them unless there is sufficient pressure to do so. Even then, we may lack the necessary knowledge to take the appropriate corrective steps. Again, if our own recent history is an accurate guide, most governmental actions will be too little and too late. A passive "solution," then, indeed seems risky. Yet it appears to be precisely the one that is in store for us. Therefore matters of policy must be squarely faced.

POLICIES RELATING TO MINORITIES
IN OTHER COUNTRIES

Americans are naturally more concerned about our own minorities than those throughout the world. Yet we have found repeatedly that what seem to be remote foreign problems suddenly explode into international crises. Americans can ill afford the luxury of turning inward in the face of these worldwide phenomena. Yet we tend to hear about them only when foreign situations become desperate or when our own interests are directly at stake. A well-informed American public is essential, but this alone will not be sufficient without institutional mechanisms that do something to help aid vulnerable world minorities and assist them in strengthening their political and economic positions.

Two very powerful American Actors in these situations are our own government and American businesses, including many multinational corporations. The former has often supported foreign governments primarily on the basis of expediency, whereas the latter have been primarily concerned with their own profits, often at the expense of standards of living within host countries. As a result, many foreign minorities continue to serve as sources of cheap labor and are often controlled politically by governments that hide behind the rationale that tight controls are necessary to prevent a communist takeover.

Sometimes the policies of these governments have been blatantly racist, as in South Africa and the former government of Rhodesia. In others such as Brazil minorities are officially nonexistent but "coincidentally" happen to form the backbone of the unskilled labor force. In all these instances it would be absurd to claim that responsibility rests entirely on American capitalist ventures or our own government. Yet each has at the very least been guilty of looking the other way in connection with the treatment of these minorities. American citizens, too, seem much more concerned that the prices of coffee, sugar, or oil be kept as low as possible than that the people who produce these commodities—often abused minorities—somehow be protected.

Perhaps an explicit effort to place minority governmental representatives in key policy positions vis-a-vis these other countries will be an important step, provided that we select individuals who are sufficiently courageous to criticize our own policies and those of friendly governments whenever appropriate. President Carter's appointment of Andrew Young, a black, to the United Nations ambassadorship was an important step in this direction, and our standing among black African nations gained considerably as a result. But Young's outspokenness cost him his job, and American credibility suffered as a result.

Governmental staff who are sensitized to minority problems in other countries are thus crucial to an enlightened foreign policy. But they are not sufficient. Many policies become subject to scrutiny only decades after they have taken effect. Sometimes we become aware of them only as a result of an energetic press or an accumulation of events within the countries themselves. We then learn about previously secret arrangements with dictatorial governments, businesses, or individuals who have been especially useful to our own government. The treatment of minorities in these countries is almost always ignored in these arrangements, even if well known to our own government.

Given this tendency for governments to follow the expedient course, which often works to the disadvantage of relatively powerless groups in other countries, what kinds of opposing forces can be mobilized? Obviously, an alert press is essential, as are legal safeguards to prevent secret governmental abuses under the guise of "national security." Important too are watchdog organizations to document and publicize instances in which governmental policies are working against the interests of minorities throughout the world. It is also crucial that our own minorities develop interests in these issues, so that they play a much more active role in policing governmental policies. Blacks are beginning to do this with respect to the African continent. Our Hispanic minorities would seem to have a parallel interest in connection with Central and Latin America.

Similar steps must be taken to monitor the largest corporations that now carry out diversified economic activities throughout the world. Insofar as these rely heavily on cheap labor to extract raw materials and fail to return adequate investments in these countries, they are obviously contributing disproportionately to the poor economic condition of those whose labor they pay so little for. Some host governments openly support this kind of extractive arrangement by private enterprise, since members of the small ruling classes are often the beneficiaries.

Sooner or later, hatred toward these elites tends to boil over, and along with it there is a resentment not only toward the corporations taking part in the economic partnership but also toward the American government. The troublesome situation brought about in the early 1980s by our support of the Shah of Iran was only one among many such potentially explosive mixtures. Support of the repressive regime in South Korea has been another, as has been our endorsement of similar governments in the Philippines and many Latin American countries. Motivating this support is not only a concern for political stability but also for economic profits as well.

The fact that the populations in these countries are usually nonwhite may make it more difficult for white Americans to modify negative stereotypes of these peoples and easier to rationalize their poverty in racial or ethnic terms. By the same token, our apparent lack of concern about their fate serves to reinforce anti-white and anti-American stereotypes among Third World peoples. It will be a long time before the resentment subsides in these countries. The American public needs to be made more aware of our own responsibilities in this connection.

POLICIES RELATING TO AMERICA'S INTERNAL MINORITIES

If one looks at overall trends during the past century, there can be no question that both the absolute and relative positions of virtually all of our domestic minorities have been improving. The *rate* of improvement, however, has been uneven and far too slow to satisfy those most immediately affected. Changes during the first half of this period, from 1880 to roughly 1930, were very slow. Actual violence against blacks and American Indians subsided during this half-century, but their economic positions improved hardly at all. Although many white ethnic minorities began to use their votes effectively, this did not prevent a resurgence of anti-Catholic and antiimmigrant hostility during the 1920s. Despite the suffering brought on by the Great Depression of the 1930s, that economic collapse had at least one important indirect effect in the growth of a vigorous labor movement under the protective policies of President Roosevelt's New Deal program. Our black and Hispanic minorities, as well as virtually all American Indians, were only to profit from these developments a decade or so later.

Following World War II, continued prosperity and rising black militancy set in motion a series of legal, political, and economic changes. There is no question that the economic improvements experienced by these groups have been considerable, but whether minorities have been gaining ground in comparison with whites depends on how one measures these groups' relative positions. Although the relative gains in minority economic and social status therefore remain controversial, their legal and political gains have indeed been profound.

Thus, progress has been uneven and has been more difficult to achieve than all but the most pessimistic social analysts would have predicted a century ago. This of course raises the important question of whether we may expect these changes to continue, and if so at what pace. Is it not possible that there will be severe reversals, particularly in the economic sphere?

It would be comforting to believe that a capitalistic system, coupled with a democratic form of government, will automatically adjust itself and continually make improvements so that domestic minorities will become fully integrated into our economy, given their proportionate share of good jobs, and protected from discriminatory policies. It would also be convenient to believe that our economy can always absorb into the labor force all those who wish to work.

There seems to be little reason to suppose, however, that a system that is primarily oriented to profit for investors and management and to high wages for workers who can command them will also be one that assures satisfactory jobs and a reasonable level of living for minorities who either lack resources to compete or are handicapped by discrimination. What mechanisms can assure that labor supply and labor demand are continually balanced? In the past, whatever "balance" has occurred resulted from a combination of an expanding economy and our ability to attract immigrants from other countries. Often, the balancing act has been accompanied by considerable labor tension, restrictive immigration policies, or the opportunistic use of cheap labor.

As the rate of economic expansion slows down, and as automation results in capital-intensive industries in which unskilled labor is redundant, we will be fortunate if a satisfactory "balance" occurs solely through economic market mechanisms. Therefore, if the positive features of a capitalistic economy are to be preserved, our system must be supplemented by other forces that are more sensitive to the needs of minority citizens, as well as the many members of our white majority near the bottom of the economic ladder.

Apart from the programs of our federal, state, and local governments, what complementary mechanisms can we find? As yet, no one has found a satisfactory answer. The danger is that very few may be motivated to try until tension levels have again become too high. And when they do rise to intolerable levels, programs that might have earlier seemed constructive may be defeated because they are too controversial for many, too inadequate for others, and too delayed in their consequences to resolve problems of crisis proportions. At such a point we may be in deep trouble.

From the standpoint of economic policies the only constructive resolution would appear to be to rely on extensive governmental programs designed not only to pick up the slack during downturns in economic cycles but also to provide long-term opportunities for minorities outside the private sector. At the same time, there must also be a series of vigorously enforced protective policies to assure minorities that discriminatory practices will be prevented.

Recent governmental policies have been moving in both these directions, but with insufficient consistency to assure genuine progress. That such policies will be implemented to any greater degree in the near future is highly questionable, and many signs point in the reverse direction. Although some city governments have been sufficiently influenced by large minority votes to take such actions, they have simultaneously found their efforts eroded by their growing economic problems. State governments seem reluctant to provide economic assistance to their minority residents, and our federal government has increasingly been under pressure to reduce its own role in this regard. Thus, from the standpoint of our lower-status minorities, the picture does not look encouraging.

Minority unemployment and underemployment have become especially pronounced as a result of our capitalistic economy's trend away from heavy reliance on cheap agricultural and industrial labor. Given a steady influx of Hispanic immigrants—many who would once have filled just those jobs that today's technological advances are eradicating—the prognosis is that this problem will remain serious over at least the next two or three decades. It therefore seems essential that governments at all three levels address this problem.

The notion that a six to eight percent unemployment rate is necessary to prevent runaway inflation seems to be gaining acceptance, but the economic theories upon which such assumptions have been based should not be taken as the final word. Yet they provide a convenient rationale for conservative policies regarding the unemployment situation. The solution to this problem, if there is one, will depend on governmental policies that encourage the expansion of the public sector to create additional jobs to fill the void produced by changes in the private sector and the general labor-force composition. In particular, new jobs must be created to compensate for the growing numbers of white women who elect to enter the labor force and whose competitive position is superior to that of many minority workers.

Not only must we create new jobs, but we must also see to it that existing positions are filled in an equitable way. Affirmative-action programs have received considerable criticism on the grounds that they are unfair to white males, but we must remember that they were instituted precisely because it is extremely easy for employers, educational institutions, or labor unions to discriminate against minorities and women, either by claiming that few "qualified" minorities or women ever apply or by protesting that only they, and not outsiders, can assess who qualifies for employment.

What affirmative-action requirements have done is to apply pressure on such "gatekeepers" by telling them that if they do not play an active role in locating the best-qualified minority applicants, then they—rather than the minorities—will have to pay a price. As long as such affirmative-action programs do not become overly rigid and absurd, they will remain an effective tool in assisting minorities to gain access to occupations in which they have been hitherto almost totally absent. Unless these minorities possess genuine competitive resources, however, affirmative-action programs alone cannot have more than a token impact on their overall career opportunities.

What are the options for American minorities? Clearly, it is essential for each minority to find a way to socialize its members so that they may obtain the competitive resources necessary to achieve genuine self-respect. Somehow, this must be accomplished in spite of the fact that most of our minorities, for a long time to come, will find themselves with below-average incomes, in relatively low-status occupations, living under overcrowded housing conditions, and continually subjected to at least moderate degrees of discrimination and personal rebuffs. Each minority must also accomplish this feat without retreating inward and, in effect, isolating itself from the majority group as well as other minorities. Yet, to be realistic, we cannot expect minorities to play this difficult role without reacting in ways that sometimes work to their own long-run disadvantage.

Thus we must expect all but the tiniest minorities to move ambivalently between pluralist—or even separatist—resolutions, on the one hand, and integrationist ones, on the other. Each will develop a set of separate institutions—such as churches, voluntary organizations, and businesses—providing the opportunities and protections that will enable the development of an autonomous minority leadership capable of taking action on the part of the minority. At the same time, however, these very same leaders are apt to have vested interests in these segregated institutions and, therefore, cannot necessarily be counted on to help the minority work toward an integrationist resolution. Thus there is a delicate balance between the desirability of pluralist-separatist programs that encourage the growth of self-reliance and minority leadership and the ultimate objective of making the minority an integral part of the larger society. A minority that moves too far in the first direction may find itself in perpetual or sporadic conflict with the majority. Such a minority may remain in a disadvantaged position for a long period of time.

THE LONG ROAD TO AN EQUITABLE SOCIETY

It has become fashionable to stress cultural pluralism as a way out of the dilemma of racial and ethnic inequalities. "Pluralism," however, means different things to different people. To the extent that its meaning is interpreted as involving a mutual appreciation for cultural differences, along with a resolve to protect each group's right to maintain its own way of life, few can quarrel with the notion. There are a number of important kinds of cultural differences, however, that also produce conflicts and that perpetuate inequalities among groups. For example, linguistic differences, such as those that exist in Belgium and Canada, not only make it difficult to avoid an economic division of labor that gives the advantage to one language group over the other, but they perpetuate all sorts of inconveniences in communication. Likewise, extreme cultural differences of the sort that exist among many neighboring groups in black Africa often lead to protracted conflicts.

The most workable model of a pluralist society has been Switzerland, and conceivably our own system could be modeled after some of its features. Historically, the Swiss federation came about through a series of coalitions among internally homogeneous but externally very distinct communities or cantons. To appreciate the pluralism of today's Switzerland, consider that residents of its various cantons derive from French, German, Italian, and several other distinct cultures. The continuation of this working relationship has, however, required a degree of decentralization that hardly seems workable in the case of a major power. Furthermore, not all Swiss cantons are equally prosperous. The Italian-speaking canton of Ticino is far less industrialized than the cantons of Bern, Zurich, or Geneva. The Swiss have also relied on rigid immigration quotas and migratory labor arrangements that have protected the French- and German-speaking cantons from an influx of permanent immigrants from Italy and Eastern Europe while assuring the country of a cheap source of labor when needed. Likewise, discontent has arisen in "backwater" areas of the German-speaking canton of Bern, where predominantly rural and French-speaking Swiss from the Jura region were in open rebellion for over a decade.

It is not at all clear, then, that a pluralistic solution can persist without the aid of rather unusual protective devices of one sort or another. A closer look at the Swiss model may, however, suggest a number of mechanisms that might be imported into other countries. One key ingredient for pluralism to succeed seems to be territorial segregation into reasonably homogeneous units, with a high degree of autonomy afforded to each such unit. Another seems to be an extensive series of cultural and political mechanisms that encourage compromise resolutions through which winning sides offer substantial compensations to the losers, so that there are no parties with major grievances. This model offers our country an urgent conclusion: if American society is ever to attain such a state of affairs, there will need to be a series of major white-majority concessions to our internal minorities.

We have noted that the basic dilemma faced by all minorities is that of increasing their resource and mobilization levels without producing a countermovement within the more powerful dominant group. A carefully controlled conflict strategy, such as that conducted during the early stages of the Civil Rights movement, may have this effect. The aim of that movement, presumably, was to encourage racial pride among blacks while stimulating the consciences of whites so that a sufficiently large number of liberals might join blacks to form a meaningful coalition. Such a coalition did materialize and was strong enough to pass important federal legislation. But it was not powerful enough to make a sizeable dent on occupational and income inequalities. Partly as a result of the disillusionment stemming from this latter failure, some blacks then began to take a more conflict-oriented stance that ultimately produced a weakening of this coalition.

White Americans must come to recognize the cruel dilemmas faced by relatively weak parties. On the one hand, considerations of fair play demand that *rapid* progress toward genuine equality of opportunity be achieved. Yet the only way that minorities seem to be able to call their situation to the attention of the American public is through dramatic actions that often generate animosities. If such intergroup conflicts reoccur at rather frequent intervals, a history of grievances and hatreds develops that makes it increasingly difficult to define competition along any other lines. Sharp dichotomies between groups then develop, and incident feeds upon incident until the conflict becomes difficult to bring under control.

Thus a conflict strategy, if it is not to get out of hand, can only be applied at appropriate times and cannot be expected to lead to immediate and dramatic gains. But, unfortunately, a "strategy" of patience and cooperation with the majority can only, at best, be expected to lead to a slow rate of improvement (unless the minority in question already possesses the necessary competitive resources, as did our Japanese-American minority after World War II). Therefore a low-status minority is seldom in a position to achieve rapid gains, regardless of the strategy it may employ.

The greatest hope for a *reasonably* rapid rate of progress for American minorities seems to revolve around their ability to form effective coalitions with each other and with whatever fraction of the liberal-white population is willing to work with them. Thus far, cooperation among American minorities has been minimal. Absolutely essential is a higher degree of cooperation between blacks and the several Hispanic minorities that are, themselves, poorly coordinated. The tendency for each of these minorities to form its own separate programs and organizations has led to a situation in which each minority sees its own problems as unique. In some instances it has also led to disputes among minorities as to the relative slice of the economic pie that each is to receive. Presumably, educational programs and pan-minority organizations that can help members of different minorities to better understand each other will eventually improve these relationships. But we appear to be a long distance from achieving an effective political or economic coalition even between blacks and Hispanics; nor is there reason to expect that this will, given time, inevitably occur. On the contrary, if our economy contracts and if immigration from Mexico continues unabated, these two minorities may find themselves in severe competition for a diminishing number of jobs.

FINAL REMARKS

Anyone who studies the history of interracial and interethnic relations cannot help but be impressed by the magnitude and persistence of the problems they involve. It is also difficult to be optimistic, either about "human nature" or the social institutions that we have thus far constructed. Yet, over the long run there are some encouraging signs, particularly within our own country. Perhaps the main point to emphasize is that the future is very much in doubt. Our minorities may find themselves in a considerably improved situation several decades from now, or they may be in a hellish one. We may see a gradual integration of these minorities into American society, in the sense that their educational, occupational, income, and residential patterns come to look very much like those of the majority. Or we may begin a downward spiral toward increasing conflict and even guerrilla warfare, coupled with growing segregation and a rigidified occupational system that serve to place severe pressures on our democratic form of government.

Though by no means sufficient in itself, we need an enlightened American public that is sensitized to the problems faced not only by our own internal minorities but also by similar groups throughout the world. Thus it is crucial that the relationships among racial and ethnic groups be subjected to continuous scrutiny, rather than conveniently swept under the rug. It is also important that each of these problems be carefully studied so that the major causal mechanisms can be better understood.

Ultimately, however, not even greater public awareness or increased scientific understanding will be sufficient. Policies and programs must be implemented which assure minorities that they will not only be protected from the more powerful majority—when it is motivated to act against their interests—but will also be encouraged to develop autonomously and to become an integral part of the larger social systems in which they happen to find themselves. Thus we are faced with an important but difficult challenge. It remains to be seen whether we will be motivated to meet it and what will happen if we do not.

INDEX

T

Taeuber, Alma F., 90, 100
Taeuber, Karl E., 90, 100
Taylor, Howard, 85
Territorial base, 106
Territorial claims, 87–88
Thomas, Dorothy S., 9
Thomas, Gail E., 74, 84
Thomas, Robert J., 47
Trieman, Donald J., 83
Tribute systems, 36

U

Unemployment, 3, 41, 64, 77, 122
United Farm Workers, 104
Unskilled labor, 35, 41, 63
Urbanization, 63
Utilities, 24, 43–46, 103
    subjective expected, 16–19, 23, 25

V

van den Berghe, Pierre L., 45, 47, 48
Vander Zanden, James W., 47
Van Doren, Charles, 116
Varience, 25, 83

Violence, 60–62, 112–15

W

Wagley, Charles, 47, 53, 62, 66, 67
Wallerstein, Immanuel, 47, 48
Warner, W. Lloyd, 66
Watson, Tom, 56
Weed, J. A., 100
Welfare, social, 78
Wilcox, Jerry, 84
Wilken, Paul H., 24, 25, 47, 115
Willhelm, Sidney, 41, 47
Williams, Eric, 9, 34, 47
Williams, Lea E., 9
Williams, Robin M., Jr., 25
Wilson, William J., 108, 116
Withdrawal, 106, 108 (*see also* Segregation)
Woodward, C. Vann, 56, 67
Wright, Eric Olin, 75, 76, 84

Y

Yancey, William L., 85
Yinger, J. Milton, 100
Young, Andrew, 120